The Bewitched

a play by

PETER BARNES

HEINEMANN

LONDON

Heinemann Educational Books Ltd
LONDON   EDINBURGH   MELBOURNE   AUCKLAND   TORONTO
HONG KONG   SINGAPORE   KUALA LUMPUR
IBADAN   NAIROBI   JOHANNESBURG
NEW DELHI

ISBN 0 435 23061 1 (cased)
435 23062 x (paperback)

Published by
Heinemann Educational Books Ltd
48 Charles Street, London W1X 8AH
Printed in Great Britain by
Morrison and Gibb Ltd, London and Edinburgh

CONTENTS

THE BEWITCHED

ACKNOWLEDGEMENTS

The lyrics of 'Lucky in Love', copyright © 1927 by Harms Inc., are reproduced by permission of Chappell & Co., Ltd; words and music by Buddy G. De Sylva, Lew Brown and Ray Henderson. This was originally from the show *Good News*.

The lyrics of 'Clap Your Hands' are reproduced by courtesy of Warner Bros. Music Ltd.

It has not been possible in all cases to trace the copyright holders of lyrics. The publishers would be glad to hear from any such unacknowledged copyright holders.

INTRODUCTION

'The lights go up on Philip IV of Spain in his shrouded bed-chamber . . .' I can confess now that I read the first stage-direction of Peter Barnes's *The Bewitched* with a sinking heart. I had looked forward to its arrival on my desk as the first ray of sunshine in a long, dry-as-dust winter in the script department of the Royal Shakespeare Company. For most of the past year, it seemed to me, I had been writing letters explaining gently that the RSC's devotion to the Bard did not extend to blank verse, five-act tragedies he had inexplicably failed to write himself about Henry I, Edward III, Lambert Simnel and Diane de Poitiers. It seemed impossible to persuade playwrights that a diet of Shakespeare's chronicles and Roman history plays did not leave our actors hungering to appear in forty-character pageants set during the Norman invasion, Monmouth's Rebellion and the Napoleonic Wars. What we wanted, I would try to explain, were plays of Elizabethan scope and theatricality, but essentially modern in their tone and stagecraft, relevant to the concerns of Britain today—the sort of model I had in mind was Peter Barnes' *The Ruling Class*. And now, after four years, Peter had finally written a new play and offered it specially to the RSC, swarming with cardinals, Grand Inquisitors and dwarfs, dealing with the last and most obscure of the Spanish Hapsburgs, a monarch whose only significance was that his death caused the War of the Spanish Succession and that 'famous victory' by Marlborough at Blenheim. If old Caspar in Southey's poem a hundred years later couldn't remember what that battle was all about, what on earth would Carlos II of Spain mean to audiences in the second half of the twentieth century?

All of which is a warning to play-readers, myself at their head, against doctrine, relevance-chasing and preconceived ideas. Several hours later, I finished reading *The Bewitched* for the second time and typed a memorandum to Trevor Nunn, the RSC's artistic director, beginning: 'God must love us after all. I think this is a work of genius.' Simply, *The Bewitched* was the finest modern play I'd read in years: the most extraordinary, the most theatrical and—yes, but without a single nudge or sidelong glance at the audience—the most pertinent to British society in the 1970s. It imposed itself with the feeling of a classic; but this wasn't only because it spoke, as the greatest Elizabethan and Jacobean plays do, to modern concerns in a seventeenth-century accent. I knew I was in the presence of something remarkable because, in scene after scene, it led me over ground no playwright had trodden before, to climax after climax of a daring which defined you to imagine how it could ever be staged. Time and again, it produced the effect which A. E. Housman called the one infallible test of poetry: it made my scalp prickle with cold excitement.

Another sign of a major work of art is that it should bring together, crystallized within a single image or statement, tendencies which have appeared, apparently unconnected, in other works preceding it. In the literature of the 1830s, for example, there is a strain of apparently groundless terror and foreboding which links works as disparate as Tennyson's 'Locksley Hall', Dickens' *Barnaby Rudge* and Bulwer-Lytton's *Last Days of Pompeii*. In Carlyle's *French Revolution* their vague fears and intimations of apocalypse acquire a focus and name: this, you realize, was the great doom hanging over the early Victorian imagination. Similarly, in the British drama of the 1960s, a new tone of comedy and disillusion seems to raise its head. In the black farce of Joe Orton, the metaphysical wit of Tom Stoppard, the Goyescan horror of Edward Bond's *Early Morning* and *Lear*, there is a common note which one could only, at the time, describe loosely as Jacobean—a sense of things falling apart, a bitter delight in their new randomness, an appalled disgust at the superstition and brutality revealed by the collapse of the old order, which brought to mind Ben Jonson, Donne and

Webster. By comparison, the playwrights of the 1950s—John Osborne, Arnold Wesker—seemed like survivals from a more confident, neo-Elizabethan age: isolated Raleighs offended by the new era's lack of respect for language, craft, the principle of merit.

Peter Barnes gathers all these threads together in *The Bewitched*. It is a neo-Jacobean play which crystallizes, clarifies and pins down what it is that links the Jacobeans and his contemporaries. Partly, it does so by being genuinely Jacobean in thought and texture: only a writer saturated as Barnes is in the language of Jonson, Marston and Middleton (he has taken time out from his own career to edit *The Alchemist*, *The Devil is an Ass*, and *Antonio and Mellida* for contemporary audiences) could have produced the brilliant, thorny, fantastic speech of Carlos' courtiers, the two great verse tirades the stammering king speaks in the lucid aftermath of epilepsy. But more than that, it penetrates to the heart of the Jacobean melancholy which is also our own: the discovery that 'the new philosophy casts all in doubt', that the universe is absurd and all the comforting beliefs in which we were reared are frantic constructs to mask this intolerable truth.

'Blind chance rules the world!' cry the possessed nuns of Cangas in the astonishing exorcism scene in Barnes's second act. Theirs are the only sane voices in a society which has organized itself insanely in order to shelter itself from such knowledge. As protection against the unbearable notion of an inane universe, the greatest empire the world had seen until the rise of our own clung to belief in the magic power of one almost inane human being, the rule of a king who could not digest his food, control his bladder or put words together consecutively. Carlos II was probably the most tragic consequence history has seen of the faith in a sacred caste of divinely appointed rulers. Because royalty could mate only with royalty, king's children with king's children, generations of Hapsburg cousins had interbred to produce a man who inherited madness from twenty-three of his ancestors, in whom the notorious Hapsburg jaw was so

B—I*

pronounced that he could not chew. For nearly thirty years, the whole of Spain and Europe hung on the spectacle of this unfortunate creature trying to engender an heir who might sustain the vast hierarchy of values and privileges which hinged on him. As John Nada comments in the most recent biography of Carlos, 'Nobody can understand how powerful over the human mind the belief in the divinity of kings can be, unless he has watched its effects where the king has been an idiot.'

But *The Bewitched* is no more a play about monarchy than *The Ruling Class* (despite fairly general critical misconception) was a play about aristocracy. What makes it bitingly relevant to Britain in the 1970s is its scathing examination of the belief that any category of people, royal or not, is 'special': peculiarly fitted to govern empires, occupy positions of privilege, command more wealth than others. Carlos was only important to Spain because his 'divinity' sanctioned the special position of tier after tier of nobles, clerics and civil servants within the pyramidal society he crowned. As Carlos himself sees in the luminous clarity of post-epilepsy, the enemy is Authority:

No blessings come from 't,
No man born shouldst ha' t' wield 't.
Authority's the basilisk, the crowned dragon,
Scaly, beaked and loathsome.
Born from a cock's egg, hatched under a toad,
Its voice is terror, glance, certain death.
Streams where 't drank once are poisoned
And the grass around turns black.
'Twill make a desert o' this world
Whilst there's still one man left t' give commands
And another who'll obey them.

Or to give it its contemporary name, the principle of merit. As *The Bewitched* shows, with no manipulation of historical fact to make its case, Spain was not ruled by Carlos but by such men as Pontocarrero, Cardinal of Toledo and head of the imperial bureaucracy, who owed their positions to their own skills and brain-power and upheld the monarchy only for the aura of sacredness it reflected on their own authority. The most striking difference between the British playwrights of the Sixties and their predecessors of the Osborne generation is that they, the neo-Elizabethans, saw themselves as forerunners of a merito-cratic revolution, an opening by universal education of all careers to the talents, which would create a new aristocracy of mind, rather than birth or inherited wealth. Peter Barnes and his contemporaries challenge that definition of equality, satirizing with grim Jacobean wit the society meritocracy has built. So that the title of *The Bewitched* spreads beyond the unfortunate Carlos 'el Encantado', beyond the sleepwalking empire which collapsed about him, to the ghost-empire we in Britain inhabit now, with its dreams of supersonic supremacy, its chauffeur-driven executive Bentleys, its newspapers whose favourite editorial verb is 'must' and its ever-soaring sterling deficits. 'Bewitchment's the cause of our present ills,' explains Father Froylan, the royal confessor, to Carlos, 'it holds us in dream.' Spain's dream, as Peter Barnes has written it, is our nightmare, pinned down and crystallized. It would be pleasant to think that his mocking, despairing laughter might still wake us.

RONALD BRYDEN

To Ron

CAST OF FIRST LONDON PERFORMANCE

The Bewitched was first presented at the Aldwych Theatre on 7 May 1974 with the following cast:

NUN/LADY IN WAITING	*Madeline Bellamy*
NUN/LADY IN WAITING	*Edwina Ford*
BELEPSCH	*Janet Henfrey*
THERESA	*Dilys Laye*
NUN/LADY IN WAITING	*Joan Morrow*
QUEEN ANA	*Rosemary McHale*
QUEEN MARIANA	*Elizabeth Spriggs*
LADY IN WAITING	*Valerie Verdun*
ALBA	*Tim Buckland*
SEBASTIEN DE MORRA/RAFAEL DE MORRA	*George Claydon*
MONTERREY	*Lee Crawford*
PHILIP IV/VALLADARES	*Mark Dignam*
SINGER	*Philip Doghan*
GONGORA	*Peter Geddis*
TORRES	*Patrick Godfrey*
CARLOS	*Alan Howard*
GOMEZ	*Christopher Jenkinson*
DR GELEEN	*Sidney Livingstone*
PONTOCARRERO	*Philip Locke*
REBENAC	*Walter McMonagle*
ANTONIO	*Phillip Manikum*
OLD MAN	*Joe Marcell*
FROYLAN	*Joe Melia*
MONK/ATTENDANT	*Michael Mellinger*
MONK/ATTENDANT	*Anthony Nash*
RAFAEL DE MORRA/SEBASTIEN DE MORRA	*Peter O'Farrell*
DURO/TENDA	*Trevor Peacock*
ALMIRANTE	*Nicholas Selby*
DR BRAVO	*Barry Stanton*
ASSASSIN	*Keith Taylor*
MOTILLA	*David Waller*
ALCALA	*Arthur Whybrow*

The play was directed by TERRY HANDS
Designed by FARRAH
Lighting by STEWART LEVITON

The Bewitched

LIST OF CHARACTERS

PHILIP IV OF SPAIN
CARDINAL PONTOCARRERO, *Jesuit, Archbishop of Toledo*
DUQUE DE MEDINA DE LA TORRES, *Council of State*
COUNT DE MONTERREY, *Council of State*
DUQUE DE ALBA, *Council of State*
SEBASTIEN DE MORRA, *Court jester to Philip IV*
CARLOS II OF SPAIN
RAFAEL DE MORRA, *Sebastien's son, Court jester to Carlos II*
ALMIRANTE DE CASTILLA, *Council of State*
FATHER FROYLAN, *Jesuit priest, Pontocarrero's assistant*
DR BRAVO, *Royal Physician*
OLD MAN
MOTILLA, *Dominican, Royal Confessor*
ANTONIO DE ALMINDA, *Royal Dancing Master*
DON SEBASTIEN VEGA, *Patriarch of the Indies*
HERMONYMOUS GONGORA, *Court Astrologer*
PIERRE REBENAC, *French Ambassador*
DR GELEEN, *Bravo's assistant*
ALONSO DE ALCALA, *Chief Torturer*
GOMEZ, *his son*
VALLADARES, *Dominican, Inquisitor-General*
LOPEZ DURO, *a Jew*
PEDLAR
FRIAR MAURO TENDA, *Capuchin*
PHILIP IV OF FRANCE

BEATRIZ
QUEEN MARIANA, *mother of Carlos II*
QUEEN ANA OF NEUBERG, *wife of Carlos II*
CONDESA BELEPSCH, *Ana's companion*
DONA MARIA ENGRACIA DE TOLEDO MARQUESA DE LOS VELEZE, *Royal Nurse*
THERESA DIEGO, *Head Washerwoman*
SISTER INEZ ⎤
SISTER RENATA ⎬ *Nuns of Cangas*
SISTER JUANA ⎦

LADIES IN WAITING, ATTENDANTS, MONKS, PRIESTS, PRISONERS, EXECUTIONER, MOURNERS, MESSENGERS, PEASANTS

PROLOGUE

Darkness. A funeral bell tolls.

PONTOCARRERO'S VOICE: No man dies suddenly. Death gi'es us warning. For what are the accidents and diseases o' life but warnings o' death. Now that most blessed infant, Prince Felipé, Prospero, Knight o' the Golden Fleece, heir t' the throne o' Spain, lies rotting in the House o' Corruption. Samson's hair, David's sling, Sisera's nail, Egypt's eight plagues, maketh not such sorrow. But we trust in Thy infinite mercy, Lord, and the continuing strength o' Thy representative on earth, His Most Catholic Majesty Philip IV o' Spain. . .

Lights up on PHILIP IV *of Spain in his shrouded bedchamber. Double doors Up Stage Centre, a full length mirror Stage Right. Opposite, Stage Left, a curtained four-poster bed. Below it Down Stage Left the elegant Jesuit priest,* PONTOCARRERO, *kneels in front of a small, portable altar chanting the 'Miserere' while the light from a tallow candle flickers over a crucified Christ.*

PHILIP *stands cold and aloof Down Stage Centre dressed in black: padded breeches, short cloak and doublet with a small, stiff 'golilla' lace collar, which makes it difficult for him to turn his head. The magnificent Golden Fleece insignia hangs round his neck. He has the traditional curved moustache and his chin is covered with a black silk mask.*

Kneeling on one knee by him are three Spanish grandees: the DUQUE DE MEDINA DE LA TORRES, *the* COUNT DE MONTER-REY *and the* DUQUE DE ALBA. *In contrast to the King they are dressed in brocade cloaks and doublets embroidered in gold and breeches gartered with rosettes. Insignias stud their chests and their gloved hands glitter with rings. Each grandee carries a black velvet cushion.*

TWO ATTENDANTS *in black stand behind* PHILIP *whilst a*

bearded dwarf, SEBASTIEN DE MORRA *dressed exactly like the grandees sits perched on the single chair by the bed.*

Taking care not to actually touch him, the ATTENDANTS *swiftly take off Philip's cloak doublet and insignia and lay them on* ALBA'S *cushion. Bowing frequently, he exits backwards Up Stage Centre.* PHILIP *lifts his legs stiffly. His heel-less shoes are removed and placed on* MONTERREY'S *cushion. He, too, exits backwards, bowing.* PHILIP'S *breeches are pulled off and placed on* TORRES'S *cushion. He exits like the others.* PHILIP *is left in his dirty grey drawers and vest. His gnarled body is painfully twisted, his arms and legs pock-marked with sores.*

ALBA *returns solemnly carrying a nightshirt on his cushion. He drops onto one knee in front of* PHILIP, *who lifts up his arms. The* ATTENDANTS *slip the nightshirt on him.* MONTERREY *re-enters with two curved pomaded leather covers which, as he kneels, are picked up and placed over Philip's moustache. Finally* TORRES *comes back carrying a chamber pot embossed with the Royal Coat of Arms. Kneeling, he holds it up expectantly in position. The* ATTENDANTS *lift Philip's nightshirt, but as there is no response from the King, they take the pot from a disappointed* TORRES *and place it beside the bed.*

PONTOCARRERO *stops chanting the 'Miserere'. The* ATTEN-DANTS *exit backwards, bowing.* PHILIP *holds out his hand and the grandees kiss it in turn before retiring like the* ATTENDANTS.

PONTOCARRERO *crosses with an open Bible;* PHILIP *kisses it and the priest follows the grandees out. Finally the dwarf* MORRA *jumps down off the chair, bows solemnly and exits backwards like the others, only in a series of dignified back-somersaults.*

There has been no reaction from PHILIP *throughout the entire ritual undressing. Hobbling to the altar, he lowers himself to his knees and gravely strikes his forehead against the altar rail.*

PHILIP: Lord, I suppeth up sin as' t were water. My lust corrupts the age. Troops o' virgins passed under me; ripe lips bathed in rancid grease, pink bodies smelling o' perfume and sweet waters t' cover the stench from their wrinkled thighs and armpits. And f' these delights I'm damned. *Punish me Lord, punish me.* As the Apostles gave thanks after the whippings and the children were joyful i' the furnace, so I will rejoice in my pain. *Crucify me Lord, crucify me.* But only Spain is crucified. Felipé's dead. As he was my beloved son, I rejoice in my punishment. As he was Spain's future King I weep at her loss. . . . Oh Blessed Virgin, Lady o' Angels, Joy o' Saints, Gate o' Paradise, make the Queen fruitful tonight. Tip my lance, plant my seed, that another son may be born t' inherit this Thy Kingdom. Amen. . . . (*Crossing himself he snuffs out the candle, hauls himself up and moves to the mirror.*) Two wives, thirty-eight bastards, 1,244 liaisons not counting one-night bawds, and I've t' pray t' God t' raise up my plug-tail. Before I only prayed t' Him t' keep it down. (*He takes off his mask to reveal the famous protruding Hapsburg jaw covered with livid sores.*) *The women, the women.* The rustle o' petticoats and farthingales i' the sun, the touching, poking, prying, licking i' the shadows—*there, there.* Old man's dreams. 'Tis the Spanish disease, dreaming. My people dream o' cheap bread, my captains o' great victories, my grandees o' new honours: who'll cut my meat, dust my footstool, wipe my buttocks. I dream too; o' times past, heart's ease. O' the days hunting deer in the Aranjuez and wild boar in the Prado and the nights hunting softer game along the Calle Major. And when the sky lightened 'yond the trees o' St Germino, musicians played. . . .

A pearly grey light comes up and a base-lute and viol play a courtly 'Pavan'. PHILIP *bows gravely to his image in the mirror and begins the stately dance, formally advancing and retreating.* . . .

The music changes. Lute and viol fade as guitars take up the exotic rhythms of the 'Sarabanda'. PHILIP *bows gaily to the mirror and this time the 'image' steps out of the frame: it is a beautiful young woman,* BEATRIZ, *in a thin, white nightdress. With long gliding steps and flamboyant gestures the two white figures dance, reaching a climax with* BEATRIZ *dropping on one knee as the music ends.*

PHILIP *bends down to raise her, and grunts in pain. He is a sick man again. They cross to the chair. He sits;* BEATRIZ *crouches at his feet and he strokes her hair.*

PHILIP: Tonight I do sheet-duty wi' the Queen. One last assault on Eve's custom house where Adam made his first entry. No sin in't for 't will be no pleasure. A King who dies w'out an heir betrays his kingdom and his God. He leaves behind a hole in nature, and holes must be filled, eh Beatriz? Else they destroy the world.

BEATRIZ (*breathing deeply*): Eeeeeeeeh.

PHILIP (*he lifts his arm*): Raising my arm thus 's an act o' Will, raising my plug-tail 'll be an act o' faith. Yet in my youth he stood up f' me. He needs you t' make him dance. (BEATRIZ *rubs herself against him.*) You knew how, hot and heavy in yer hands, rubbing rolled 'tween round buttocks thighs BOLT hard HARD plunged in drop d-d-drops o' sweet juices -jui-jui-jui-j-j-j-j-*ahhhhr.*

BEATRIZ: *Eeeeeeeeehhh.*

PHILIP: I feel 't. I feel 't—look! look! *It quivers.* 'Tis not as hard as a ram's horn, nor as stout as Hercules but 'twill serve. Benedícat vos Omnipotens Deus Pater et Fílius et Spíritus Sanctus. (*He makes the sign of the cross over his crotch.*) Memories too are potent. I can make me a son, wet wi' the dew o' heaven, *bold, bold.* Only spare him Lord, for princes too die young. (*The 'Magnificat' is sung softly over.*) After my end who'll hath need t' remember me? Philip IV, 1605–1665, eldest son o' Philip III and Margaret o' Austria. During his reign there were plots in Aragon, rebellions in Catalonia, defeats at Rocroy and Roussilon, whilst Jamaica, Portugal and the Netherlands were lost. When he died there wasn't a damp eye in Madrid. Go back, sweet gypsy. . . .

He closes his eyes and concentrates. BEATRIZ *tries to cling to him but an invisible force drags her away. She struggles wildly but is pushed remorselessly backwards towards the mirror. The 'Magnificat' grows louder as she holds out her hands, imploring. But with one last*

silent cry of protest BEATRIZ *is thrust back into the mirror.*
As she vanishes the light fades slightly and there are three loud
knocks. PHILIP *heaves himself up and assumes his former marble*
gravity as the doors are opened and two Dominican MONKS
carrying incensors, their heads covered with conical penitents' hoods,
enter to the sound of the 'Magnificat'.

QUEEN MARIANA *comes in out of the darkness, in a white*
shift, with long black hair. Behind her, borne on the shoulders of two
hooded MONKS *with large tallow candles, is the skeleton of Saint*
Isidore propped upright on a bier. PONTOCARRERO *comes in*
behind them carrying a silver holy water stoup and sprinkler.

The procession crosses the bedroom, chanting. The MONKS
put the bier down Stage Right and kneel beside it whilst MARIANA
demurely takes her place beside PHILIP.

PONTOCARRERO: As we despise the corruptible body o' men,
we venerate those o' the Saints and Martyrs, their bodies being
once the temples o' the Holy Spirit which God honours them
by performing miracles in their presence. Thus these moving
bones o' the Blessed Saint Isidore ha' cured spasms, sciatica,
boils, toothache and cast out devils. Now Lord God we pray
f' another miracle. As when the dead body which was plunged
down into the sepulchre o' Elysius instantly sprung t' life
when 't touched the bones o' the prophet, so let the half-dead
instrument o' Thy servant Philip spring instantly t' life when
'tis plunged into the soft sepulchre o' the flesh o' Thy servant
Mariana. In the name o' the Father and o' the Son, and o' the
Holy Ghost.

As they chant 'Amen', MARIANA *and a creaking* PHILIP
cross to opposite sides of the bed and get in. Leaving their candles
by the bier, the MONKS *rise and join* PONTOCARRERO *who*
liberally sprinkles the bed and its impassive occupants with holy
water and intones a blessing.

PONTOCARRERO: Adjutórium nostrum in nómine Domini. Qui
fecit caelum et terram. Dóminus vobiscum. Et cum spíritu
tuo . . .

He makes the sign of the Cross and the MONKS *close the bedcurtains. Chanting triumphantly they exit followed by* PONTOCARRERO. *Their voices quickly die away.*

As the skeleton watches grimly there is the sound of heavy machinery creaking into motion from the bed. Massive wheels and screws turn laboriously and ancient pistons start pounding. The whole room shakes to a brutal thudding. It reaches a crescendo, a woman screams, Saint Isidore's skeleton jerks upright on the bier and collapses in a heap.

The scream turns into staccato cries of a woman in childbirth. They increase in intensity until drowned by a great tearing sound and the floor Down Stage Centre slowly splits apart.

Lights down to a Spot on the widening crack which seems full of dark, glutinous liquid. It stirs as something rises out of it. First a hand, then a shapeless body emerges completely wrapped in a pale, pink membrane. Hauling itself feebly out of the crack it flops onto the floor where it lies curled up tight.

A sharp slap is heard and a baby starts crying: the body stirs. A choir sings 'Gloria in Excelsis' and Spot Up Stage Centre on a throne on a rostrum with sloping side and three centre steps. PHILIP *stands proudly in front of the throne. As the wet body slithers painfully towards the throne* PONTOCARRERO *intones:*

PONTOCARRERO'S VOICE: Almighty and everlasting God whose most dearly beloved son, Jesus Christ, didst shed out o' His most precious side both water and blood f' the forgiveness o' our sins, sanctify this water t' the mystical washing away of sin, and grant that this child, now to be baptized therein, may receive the fulness o' Thy Grace and ever remain in the number o' Thy faithful and elect children through Jesus Christ our Lord, amen . . . (*The body begins to flop up the rostrum steps.*) José, Segundo, Bartalome, Ignacio, Rodriguez, Fráncisco, Salvador, Gironalla, Rafael, Vincente, Gancia, Teofilo, Sainz, Luys, Miguel, Ayala, Carlos . . . (*The body painfully hauls itself upright in front of* PHILIP.) I baptize

thee in the name of the Father and of the Son and of the Holy
Ghost.

The body bursts through its membrane to reveal PRINCE
CARLOS.

CARLOS: *Dad-a, dad-a . . .*

PHILIP *reacts in horror at the sight. He clutches his chest, utters
a despairing cry and keels over backward off the rostrum, dead.*

The funeral bell tolls again. CARLOS *bows his head, slowly
turns and solemnly sits on the throne.*

*The funeral bells change into joyful peals as crowds cheer
rapturously whilst* CARLOS *stares fixedly ahead.*

ACT ONE

A parrot screeches raucously as the bells and cheers fade out to the sound of two women arguing. The deformed CARLOS II *continues staring ahead; he has a monstrous protruding chin, lank hair, long sickly face and wet lips. He is in his thirties, slovenly dressed in stained black doublet and breeches and a dirty gollila collar.*

Harsh lights full up on the bare throne-room, 1692. Banners round the panelled walls. Doors Stage Right and Left. Throne and rostrum Up Stage Centre. TWO ATTENDANTS *either side and in front of it* MARIANA, *the Queen Mother and* QUEEN ANA OF NEU-BERG. *Her Amazon parrot is on a perch nearby.*

MARIANA *is now in her sixties, her face a thick mask of white cosmetic, framed in a nun-like cowl, her stumpy body hidden beneath a black 'sacristan' dress. A cross hangs from a rolled cord round her waist and there are large rings on her fingers.* ANA, *in her late twenties, is dressed in a dark green hooped dress with puffed sleeves and square neckline. Her bare shoulders are whitened, lips and cheeks painted red, fair hair coiled and greased. She wears heavy earrings, thick bracelets on each wrist and her fingers are covered with jewellery.*

Both hieratic figures clutch a document and argue with flat ferocity, hardly moving.

MARIANA: Cribbage-faced ape-leader.

ANA: Carbuncled crone.

MARIANA: Buss-beggar.

ANA: Cock-bawd.

MARIANA: Toad-eater.

ANA: Crab-louse.

PARROT: *Pretty Joey! Pretty Joey!*

MARIANA: Piddling German fussock. I made you a Queen; made you my son's wife.

ANA: 'Tis why I hate you, thatch-gallows.

MARIANA: And why every Spaniard hates you, moss-face.

ANA: They've hated you longer, spoon-head.

CARLOS: Aaaaa III wowowon't. *I won't die.*

MARIANA: Kings 're mortal, Carlos. They're taken too; a blow, a scratch, contagion i' the air, life seeps away.

CARLOS: III measure mmmmy breath.

ANA: Acknowledge 't Carlos, wi'out an heir only a heartbeat stops the grandson of Louis XIV, (*Crossing herself*)—'In Beélzebub príncipe daemoniórum éjicit daemónia'—being made the next King o' Spain.

CARLOS: Nnnnnn . . .

PARROT: *Stop talking when I interrupt! Pretty Joey.*

MARIANA: You must make a Will naming thy successor. We're at war with Louis, (*Crossing herself*)—'In Beélzebub príncipe daemoniórum éjicit daemónia'—but even he wouldst have t' recognize your choice.

CARLOS: Bbbbbaaaaa if I make a Will I'll DIE I know 't if I. . . .

MARIANA (*thrusting her document at him*): Secure our future, Carlos, make José o' Bavaria heir t' the throne.

ANA: 'Cause he's thy great-grandson? (*She thrusts her document at* CARLOS.) The next King must be Archduke Charles o' Austria.

MARIANA: Why, 'cause he's thy nephew and you canst claim bribe money from his father?

ANA: Carlos, your successor must be strong. Charles's backed by Austria.

MARIANA: No-one'll countenance an Austrian puppet, addlepate.

ANA: But José has nothing aback o' him.

MARIANA: 'Tis why he'll be allowed t'become King, Madam Dolt.

CARLOS: Aaaaalllow. . . ?!

MARIANA: As thou lovest me, Carlos, sign f'my sake.

ANA: I'll stop m' breath, starve myself to death.

MARIANA: Don't listen t' her promises, Carlos.

CARLOS: I wwwon't daaa die. Why Wills and such? Whaaa. . . ?

ANA: You casn't produce an heir wi' the usual instrument so you must use pen and ink.

MARIANA: Thy father didst his night duty. . . .

CARLOS: KKKKKAAAAK (*He staggers up in fury and jerks spastically down the steps.*) YOOOO say IIII'm Impo-Impo-Impo TENT TENT? Am IIII AM?

ANA (*quickly*): No, Carlos.

CARLOS: NNN't true. God loves mmm. NOT IMPO . . .

MARIANA: O' course you're not impotent Carlos, but 'tis per-plexing. You've endured nineteen years o' marriage, first t' the beautiful Queen Louisa then t' this barren witch and every night 'cept during sickness and Saints Days, you've performed thy duty. That's o'er 6,000 performances, wi'out success. Carlos you're not concentrating!

CARLOS: Ssssn't meeeeeee.

MARIANA: True. The waters o' Puertollano cured the Countess Oropesa o' sterility but you've refused to take 'em Madame.

ANA: My sisters're fertile wi'out yer stinkin' gut-water; they breed like as rabbits. The fault's not in my ovaries, Madame.

PARROT: *Bananas! Brown sugar and bananas! Crrah.*

MARIANA: Cast her off, Carlos. She's sterile.

ANA: Banish her, Carlos. She hates us.

CARLOS: WWeeeee SIN.

ANA: I see thee on Judgement Day, old woman, flung into that lake o' hot pitch and the little devils clawing thee open.

MARIANA: I see thee wi' lips torn off, tongue rooted out, walking 'neath Lucifer's great arse, eating his excrement as it falls.

CARLOS: GOD hurts f'f'f' our sins, your sssins mmmy sins, whaaa?

ANA: I smell thy polluted carcass spiked stinkin' on a dung hill.

PARROT: *Kill for Lent! Kill for Lent!*

ANA: Toads gnaw thy flesh and the little devils laugh *hee-hee-hee,*
they laugh *hee-hee-hee.*

MARIANA: I hear thy screams *aaarrhh,* mercy, mercy *aaarhh
aaarhh.*

CARLOS: Sssssins sssins sssssss.

The lights flicker.

ANA (*prowling like an animal*): Laughing *hee-hee-hee-heeeee-
heeeee.*

MARIANA (*jerking her head like a bird*): *Aaarrhh-aaarrhh-
aaarrhh.*

CARLOS (*wriggling like a snake*): *Sssss-ssssss.*

*They howl and hiss with increasing fury as the light flickers faster
and grows brighter until there is an intense flash and* ANA, MARIANA
and CARLOS *let out a loud cry and fall into epileptic fits.*

CARLOS's *head rotates and his tongue lolls out as he whirls round
on his own axis, limbs thrashing wildly.* MARIANA's *legs kick
convulsively whilst her arms thrust bolt upright, fingers clutching
the air, her teeth bared in a fixed grin.* ANA's *body jerks up and
down as she tears her dress and hits her crotch in excitement.*

The PARROT *screeches whilst the* TWO ATTENDANTS *cross
unconcerned and place sticks between the jaws of the epileptics and
then return to their places.*

The convulsions stop; the attack ends. Lights down to a Spot on
ANA, CARLOS *and* MARIANA, *now in a state of post-epileptic
automation.* CARLOS *rips off his breeches and* ANA *pulls up her
dress. As he throws himself passionately on top of her,* MARIANA
rocks back and forth moaning a lullaby and the PARROT *screeches
mockingly. Spot out.*

SCENE II

Spot up immediately Wings Left as the two dwarfs SEBASTIEN DE
MORRA *and his son* RAFAEL *enter duelling furiously with tiny
rapiers.*
They are in shirtsleeves and RAFAEL *is blindfold.*

MORRA: Engage in sixte. I disengage. You parry, quarte, I disengage, you parry sixte, I disengage, you parry octave and
riposte. Enough. (*They stop Down Stage Centre.* RAFAEL *takes
off his blindfold.*) Remember f' the quick riposte keep the point
in line during the parry. Thus. (*He shows him.*) 'Tis a pity the
King's sick the day you take my place as Court Jester.

RAFAEL: And what advice 're you gi'ing me? Fathers always gi'
advice.

MORRA: And sons n'er listen. Only this: honour the King, never
be wi'out 'Mother Bunch's Joke-Book' and ne'er refuse a
fight. Thou art a de Morra: the slightest insult—*yah*. (*He
lunges,* RAFAEL *parries.*)

RAFAEL: I take your point. I'll defend my honour and the King's
and cling t' 'Mother Bunch's Joke-Book' as 't were my
Bible.

MORRA: 'Tis, and the King's your God, your polestar. You've
been at Court long enough to know who's in, who's out.
Remember, the King's always in. Thy only call is t' entertain,
t' fill an idle hour.

RAFAEL: I believe I can do more and mix a little purpose wi' my
wit.

MORRA: Fatal. I've survived two reigns by having no purpose
'cept t' please. If thou has a message, send 't by messenger.

RAFAEL Why 're licensed fools so crabby-arsed and sour?

MORRA: 'Cause they've a low opinion o' mankind and see 't
proved daily. Stupidity stains the world. 'Tis a disease not o'
the brain but the soul: a blindness, a shunning o' the light. 'Tis

not the Great Prince, Lucifer, who scourges us but that snot-nosed, snivelling God, Stupidity. And he's ne'er defeated. I know, I've lived off him all my life.

RAFAEL: A man doesn't fight merely t' win. Wi' my wit and sword I'll try and make 't all new.

MORRA: New! You'll dine off funeral meats if you try anything new! Haven't I taught thee, audiences only want the same old tumbles. The same old snatches. And any jest must have whiskers t' give satisfaction. Mother Bunch's joke Number 127: Have you got the dispatches?

RAFAEL: No, I always walk this way. *Honk, honk.*

MORRA: Number 199: My wife's got teeth like the Ten Commandments.

RAFAEL: I know—all broken. *Honk, honk.*

    RAFAEL *leaps on* MORRA's *shoulders and they cross Wings Right, earnestly practising.*

MORRA: Master Butcher, have you got a sheep's head?

RAFAEL: No, 'tis the way I part my hair.

RAFAEL: }
MORRA: } *Honk, honk.*

    Even as they exit Wings Right, honking, lights full up on the Council Chamber.

SCENE III

The Council Chamber is dominated by a huge map of the Spanish Empire on the panelled wall Up Stage Centre. Doors Stage Left and a screen Stage Right.

There are several empty places amongst the Council members sitting stiffly in high backed chairs at a long table placed slightly diagonally Stage Centre. On one side are the DUQUES TORRES *and* ALBA.

Now white-haired, TORRES *dresses soberly and toys with a book, but* ALBA *still has on his silver cloak and breeches. Seated opposite is the* COUNT DE MONTERREY, *and the dashing, pock-marked*

ALMIRANTE DE CASTILLA nonchalantly fingering his sword handle. PONTOCARRERO, now Cardinal-Archbishop of Toledo, presides at the head of the table, Up Stage in dark gown and surplice. A large sapphire ring glistens as he strokes his pointed beard. A Jesuit Priest, FATHER FROYLAN, stands beside him with a leather pouch stuffed with State Papers: at every convenient moment he gives him some to sign.
They are all listening gravely to the Royal Physician, DR BRAVO, an imposing man in large owl-like spectacles.

DR BRAVO: Your Eminence, my Lords, last night His Majesty had another attack o' 'alfereza insensata' known as epilepsy or falling sickness; 'tis his third this month. The cause is particular foul vapours from a uterus. To cure His Majesty I used the traditional methods, drawing eight ounces o' blood from his left shoulder and administering a sneezing powder o' hellbore t' purge the brain and crushed cowslip t' strengthen 't. Plaster o' pitch and pigeon dung was put on his feet, cat-fat on his chest and a draught o' vinegar and wormwood forced down his throat.

PONTOCARRERO: And?

DR BRAVO: When I left him this morning he was still unconscious.

PONTOCARRERO: How canst tell?

DR BRAVO: The signs 're plain f' one versed in physic; he lay stretched out on the ground.

PONTOCARRERO: I've oft had audience wi' the King when he lay stretched out on the ground.

DR BRAVO: But he doesn't respond t' my promptings.

ALBA: He rarely responds t' the promptings o' princes o' blood rank, so why shouldst he respond t' you.

DR BRAVO: But he lies in his own piss-water.

MONTERREY: His Majesty daily wets his breeches, a leaky conduit runs in the family.

DR BRAVO: But his eyes 're closed!

TORRES: Tired by the weight o' Kingship.

DR BRAVO: But he *looks* senseless!

PONTOCARRERO: Is *that* all? 'Tis normal. I suggest you go examine His Majesty more closely.

Bewildered, DR BRAVO *bows, makes for the door, then suddenly stops and turns back.*

DR BRAVO: Ah, but he . . . (*He stops as they stare at him.*) Hhhhmm . . . No . . . (*He exits thoughtfully.*)

PONTOCARRERO: I cannot abide Physicians, gravediggers begin where they end.

ALMIRANTE: 'Tis true His Majesty's behaviour's become passing strange. He wants t' build a bridge on the Jarama River.

MONTERREY: There's nothing wrong wi' wanting t' build a bridge on the Jarama.

ALMIRANTE: Lengthways?

PONTOCARRERO: My Lords, I'm dismayed t' find only four members o' the Council o' State've seen fit t' attend this special meeting. The King may die. We *must* recommend an heir t' the throne. All decisions wait on this, wi'out 't Spain's impotent. Already she wastes away. Father, pluck one at random. (FROYLAN *takes out a document and hands it to him: he reads.*) From our Minister in Andulciá. 'Food is short, the harvest poor, the land unploughed and plague comes for the seventh year.' Another . . .

ALBA: Your Eminence, we've grave business t' discuss and as a true grandee and Gentleman o' His Majesty's Bedchamber, I cannot stay silent. When His Majesty was convulsed last night, Attendants placed the distemper stick 'tween his teeth. All know that privilege's been reserved f' the de Albas since the Moorish Conquest!

MONTERREY: But thou weren't even i' Madrid when His Majesty was stricken.

ALBA: I had a horse ready and coulds't've been at the King's side in an easy five hours.

ALMIRANTE: In an easy five hours His Majesty coulds't've bitten through his tongue and choked i' his own blood.

ALBA: When His Most Catholic Majesty Philip III sat in front o' his fire and a spark set his breeches alight, his royal chairmover the Duque de Bejar coulds't not be found either. But His Majesty's Attendants knew their place, etiquette was observed, the duke's privileges weren't violated.

ALMIRANTE: But His Majesty burnt t' death.

ALBA: Regrettably. But the Duque de Bejar's privileges weren't violated. Take away one privilege 'cause 'tisn't convenient, others follow. Wi'out privileges no man knows his worth. I speak f' the ancient families o' Spain when I say I'll defend my privileges t' my last breath.

MONTERREY: And I t' my last ducado. Which is what mine cost me. 127,000 f' the privilege o' being the Count de Monterrey and carrying the King's footstool.

TORRES: What's 127,000 ducados t' a wealthy man?

MONTERREY: There 're no wealthy men in Spain, only men wi' money. Now our wealth's in contracts, bonds, gold and silver coinage, not in work done, goods made.

TORRES: I've 30 charities t' support, 148 relatives and 522 servants. In Spain e'en the servants've servants. What wi' taxes and the French wars, a man can work his way up from nothing t' a state o' abject poverty. (*Touches book.*) Like Virgil, I only survive, 'Arte magistra'. I thank God f' the consolations o' literature.

MONTERREY: The consolation o' money's more durable.

ALMIRANTE (*getting up*): Your Eminence, my Lords, the cods, the cods.

He crosses to behind the screen.

MONTERREY: Go buy the Viceroyship o' Mexico as I did. (ALMIRANTE *is heard passing water behind the screen; no one takes any notice.*) 'Twill fetch 200,000 ducados but you'd double 't in one year's hard graft and extortion. In a world of tawdry values and vanishing ideals I sometimes think money's the only decent thing left.

PONTOCARRERO, *who has been signing papers, raps the table.*

PONTOCARRERO: My Lords, we're not here t' discuss money or privilege yet again. The land's barren, the treasury empty, the coinage debased. E'ery paper here confirms 't; 'tis no longer noontide. Today our task's t' try and keep the Empire intact and prevent Philip Bourbon gaining the throne f' France.

ALMIRANTE *comes back doing up his breeches.*

ALMIRANTE (*he sits*): T' thwart the French pox-carriers is the task o' every man born south o' the Pyrenees.

PONTOCARRERO: So I recommend José o' Bavaria as heir, the English, Dutch and French 'll fight t' stop Charles o' Austria gaining the Spanish throne, but only the French 'll oppose José. Wi' God's help the Triple Alliance 'll fall apart.

MONTERREY: If we choose Bavaria, Your Eminence, 'tis possible the French Alliance *might* fall. Bavaria offers 'might', Austria three million i' gold. I choose the gold.

ALBA: As a Spaniard, I see 't straight. Blood ties link us wi' Austria. What's Bavaria t' me, or me t' Bavaria, eh? eh?

TORRES: A man's judged by his friends. So are nations. Bavaria's small whilst Austria has one o' the largest libraries in the world: Cicero, Terence and the complete works o' Boethius.

ALMIRANTE: 175,000 Spaniards died at Rocroy and you talk o' the complete works o' Boethius! My lords, victories aren't won by peals o' ordnance, block carriages and muskets alone, but also the spirit o' trumpet and drum. We must defeat our enemies through our strength, not their weakness. I'm f' Charles, Austria and greatness.

The four NOBLES *raise their hands.*

NOBLES: Charles, Austria and greatness.

ALBA: And copulation, eh? (*He gets up.*) Your Eminence, my lords, the cods, the cods. (*He stomps off behind the screen.*)

ALMIRANTE: Yes, copulation's a pressing matter. 'Tis said the Archduke's a most filthy fornicator. Though that may be a lie put about by his sympathisers.

TORRES: True, but on balance, I too recommend Charles, subject t' a report on his penis-member and scrotum.

PONTOCARRERO: 'Tis certain he'd've t' satisfy the canonical conditions f' virility—erectio, introductio and emissio.

TORRES: Monsignor Albizzi and Dr Bravo'd carry out the necessary measuring and weighing o' the penis-member erect and in repose.

ALMIRANTE: 'Twill be like trying t' catch a frightened eel wi' greasy sugar tongs.

PONTOCARRERO: No matter how difficult, 't must be done if Charles 's recommended. We took the Queen's fertility on trust and she's proved barren, failing in her duty.

ALMIRANTE: We fail in ours speaking o' her so. Spain's the very birthplace o' chivalry. But now 'tis gone, laughed out by that word-pecker Cervantes and his scribblings.

TORRES: Word-pecker, sir?! Scribblings?!

LMIRANTE: When the young Queen came t' us f' help i' her first days, we cursed her f' not being Spanish or pregnant. Bad harvests or high taxes, 'tis all the fault o' Queen Ana o' Neuberg. (ALBA *is heard passing water behind the screen.*) Yet her steadfast courage doeth us honour, my lords. She grows in goodness and for her sweet honour, womanly grace . . . Crow-thumper, I speak o' the Queen!

In a sudden fury he draws his sword, charges across and jabs it through the screen. ALBA *yells with fright and the* OTHERS *jump to their feet protesting.* ALMIRANTE *pulls out his sword and brings down the screen to reveal* ALBA *holding up his breeches in front of a commode.*

They are all too busy shouting to notice the Queen Mother MARIANA *enter Stage Left, carrying a Bible.*

ALMIRANTE: You'll die f' the insult t' the Queen!

ALBA: My breeches—my honour—my sword—M-M-Ma'am!

He snaps to attention as he sees MARIANA *staring at him. The* OTHERS *become aware of her.*

All bow as she takes PONTOCARRERO'*s place at the head of the table.*

PONTOCARRERO: Ma'am, this is a solemn moment. We're honoured by thy presence.

ALMIRANTE: Your Eminence, only the King canst attend Council meetings.

PONTOCARRERO: The King's still distempered. Ma'am, 'tis the State Council's humble opinion by four hands t' one, that the Archduke Charles o' Austria be recommended heir t' the throne.

MARIANA: My son, His Most Catholic Majesty Carlos o' Spain favours José o' Bavaria as his heir.

She hands PONTOCARRERO *a note, he reads it and passes it to the* OTHERS.

MONTERREY: In all conscience, Ma'am, none here knew o' His Majesty's wishes.

MARIANA: I grow old whilst you talk.

PONTOCARRERO: Those favouring the King's choice, José o' Bavaria?

MARIANA *stares coldly at each in turn. All slowly raise their hands, except* ALMIRANTE.

ALMIRANTE: In all conscience, Ma'am, I'm still f' Charles o' Austria—and the Queen.

MARIANA: We'll remember you i' all conscience . . . Four t' one in favour o' José, Your Eminence. My lords casn't see Charles'd 've governed wi'out a Regent or Council o' State? José's pliable. (*A carbuncled* OLD MAN *rises from an empty chair where he has been hidden and hobbles towards her.*) I pray t' the Holy Virgin that my son lives, but shouldst he die we must face the darkness and *arrrx* . . .

She gasps in agony as the OLD MAN *deliberately squeezes her breast. As she leans against the table, the* OTHERS *react.*

TORRES: Your Majesty, Ma'am . . .?

MARIANA *looks up to see the* OLD MAN *exiting Stage Right, wheezing and scratching himself. He has left a silver crab-brooch pinned to her breast.*

MARIANA: Nothing. Nothing. 'Twill pass . . . nothing, 'tis nothing.

PONTOCARRERO: I thank God's mercy a decision's been reached on the succession. From 't all things can flow, we've secured the future and . . .

There is a loud knock and the Royal Confessor, the gaunt Dominican priest, MOTILLA, *strides in.*

MOTILLA (*bowing*): Ma'am. Your Eminence. My lords.

PONTOCARRERO: Father Motilla, as their Majesties' Confessor, you presume too much! You've no right here.

MOTILLA: I bear God's word.

PONTOCARRERO: Hast no sense o' shame. This 's a Council o' State. No place f' God's word.

MOTILLA: Their Majesties wished you t' be the first t' know o' God's infinite mercy.

PONTOCARRERO: Mine's limited.

MOTILLA: *The Queen is pregnant.*

MARIANA: A lie!

MOTILLA: The Queen is pregnant.

MARIANA: She's barren!

MOTILLA: The falling sickness briefly turns the sufferer's soul inside out. If they're o' the spirit 't canst bring on fleshy lusts, carnal longings: 'tis a foul part o' the disease. 'T'as been observed after their foamings, ravings and jerkings their Majesties jerk together t' some purpose.

TORRES: Julius Caesar suffered from the 'falls' too. His son Caesarium was born when he fell on Cleopatra. What a fall was that.

MOTILLA: All signs confirm conception. The Queen's not bled inward this month; her neck's warm and her back cold; she craves only 'cumbers soused i' vinegar and gooseberry fool, and milk poured on her urine floats, my lords!

PONTOCARRERO: Praise be t' God.

ALBA: No need now f' Bavaria or Austria. Spain makes her own heirs!

MONTERREY: We must send His Majesty our congratulations.

ALMIRANTE: And the Queen. 'Tis the Queen's triumph, too!

They all shout 'The Queen' excitedly and bells peal. Suddenly they stop and look apprehensively at MARIANA. *The bells stop ringing too. A long silence . . .*

MARIANA (*slowly*): We must pray f' her safe deliverance. God grant 't be a son . . .

Thankfully the bells resume ringing, the lights fade out and all exit, chanting: 'Adjutórium nostrum in nómine Domini . . .'

SCENE IV

The chanting dies away to applause. Lights up on a ballroom with the walls made up of tall mirrors.

CARLOS *is being applauded by my lords* ALBA, TORRES *and* MONTERREY *and the Royal Dancing Master,* ANTONIO DE ALMINDA, *a beribboned figure with red-buckle shoes and a long staff.* RAFAEL, *the dwarf, stands next to* DR BRAVO *who waits patiently with two drinks on a silver tray.*

CARLOS: I wooon't die now, the Queen carries my SON. All signs proclaim 'twill be a bbboy. Last night the Queen dreamed o' a hatchet, heard a raven cccroak; her saliva's YELLOW and her pulse stronger on her right wrist than thaa . . . I've proved myself King, IIII've the blood, balm, crown, sceptre and the BALLS! (*He shambles round thrusting out his crotch.*) IIII humped, jocked, rutted, clicked and shafted. Haaaaven't I the finest gap-stopper, the largest whore-pipe, the biggest penis-stick i' Spain?

TORRES: Like Atlas, Sire, you balance our world on 'ts tip.

ALBA: 'Tis Goliath!

MONTERREY: 'Tis Titan!

RAFAEL: 'Tis super-prick!

    DR BRAVO *approaches with the drinks.*

DR BRAVO: Orange or lemon cordial, Sire?

CARLOS (*looking at them suspiciously*): Whaaa the difference?

DR BRAVO: Difference? One tastes o' orange, the other o' lemon, Sire.

CARLOS: You always gi' me answers never solutions!

    He gestures impatiently and DR BRAVO *exits backwards Stage Right.*

CARLOS: Weeee hear thou hast challenged the Almirante de Castilla t' a duel, my lord Alba. (*He mimes a clumsy lunge.*) Haaa we forbid 't my lord. He'll geld thee. HHHHe's most dextrous wi' his poinard.

TORRES: And you, Your Majesty.

CARLOS: The thrust in prime 'neath the girdle's ooooour best stroke.

    The OTHERS *applaud and snigger.*

ALBA: 'Twas a matter o' honour, Sire.

CARLOS: Honour's ccccome the very peak o' fashion.

RAFAEL: Aye, Sire, thieves steal 'cause they're too honourable t' beg and beggars beg 'cause they're too honourable t' steal. All have 't, but I've ne'er truly seen 't. As a friend, show me thy honour, my lord.

ALBA (*clasping sword*): I'll show you my weapon, Sir!

RAFAEL: If 'tis as flexible as thy honour, I'll've nothing t' fear.

ALBA: Who 're you t' talk o' my honour, nick ninny.

RAFAEL: Why I'm court magician and t' amuse His Majesty, I've changed water into wine, frogs into footmen, beetles into bailiffs and made grandees out o' gobbley turkey-cocks. His Majesty's but t' ask and 'tis his . . . A black star? I pluck one thus . . . (*He mimes plucking.*) Dry water? Here . . . (*He mimes pouring.*) An honourable courtier? That's impossible even f' a great magician.

ALBA: You short-shanked nothing!

RAFAEL: No, I'm Josephus Rex.

CARLOS: JJJosephus Rex? But you art our Tom-o-Thumb. Your name's er . . . er . . . Rafael Morra.

RAFAEL: No Sire, I'm truly Josephus Rex. Jo-king.

CARLOS: Who's Jo King?

RAFAEL: I am, Sire. (*Patiently.*) Josephus . . . Jo. Rex . . . King. I am joking, *honk, honk.*

CARLOS: Jo . . .? Rex King? . . . Jooooo (*He gives an adenoidal laugh.*) Heee-ee-ee *I am joking, honk, honk.*

RAFAEL (*wryly*): *Honk, honk.*

ANTONIO (*bows*): Your Majesty, 'tis noon.

CARLOS: Etiquette must bbbe obeyed eeee on this most blessed o' days. 'Tis time f'my lesson in the dance. (*The* OTHERS *bow and are about to leave;* CARLOS *gestures.*) My lords, we graaa a favour; ssssstay.

ALBA: 'Tis a great honour, Sire!

The LORDS *step back respectfully.* ANTONIO *raps three times with his staff. A drum beats and whilst he talks he glides about in time to it.*

ANTONIO: Your Majesty, the dance is a remedy f' all natural ills, 't shakes up stagnant blood, sweats out foul vapours, purges the overcharged brain. We're conceived in a dance o' love, (*he jumps*) *saut saut petit saut*, and ushered out i' a dance o' death by a corpse de ballet, (*he mimes funeral march*) *dum dum de dum.* All nature dances; waves, trees, air in summer heat, hearts f' joy. The perfect harmony o' the dance glorifies the perfect harmony o' God's universe . . . (*He bows.*) Oui, on commence. Today, Sire, we practise the 'Pavan', again. 'Tis an antique dance, but still the courtliest o' all court dances; the dance o' Kings, Queens and noblemen, its natural authority mirroring the natural authority o' its dancers. Très bon. (*He performs as he comments.*) First the single left. On the first beat step forward swerving a little t' the left on the left foot and bend the right knee slightly. On the second beat join the right foot t' the left rising on thy toes and sinking on thy heels on the half beat. The right singles similar but starting wi' the right foot . . . Très bon. Your Majesty, as we practised. Wi' éclate, éclate.

He stands opposite CARLOS. *They make reverence. The drum beats out the time.* CARLOS's *left foot skids forward and his right knee buckles. He then swings his right foot forward, hops onto his toes and flops back. Sliding out his left foot, his right skids past it, and he is trapped in the splits. After managing to raise himself up, he pushes out his left foot, brings his right foot up to it, and keels over onto the floor with a crash.*

The COURTIERS *murmur approval.* CARLOS *looks up enquiringly at* ANTONIO.

ANTONIO (*slowly*): Hhmmm, a-l-m-o-s-t right, Sire.

CARLOS *gets up. The drum beats again as he reverses and skids about in a series of extraordinary spastic lurches, arms and legs jerking uncontrollably and ending once again on the floor.*

CARLOS: 'TTTis aaaa improvement, eh? eh?

ANTONIO (*slowly*): Yes, I think I canst say 'tis an improvement . . . (*shuddering*) remembering how it was.

CARLOS (*getting up*): III've only been practising five years.

TORRES: Your Majesty hath a natural sense o' rhythm.

RAFAEL: Sire, try that new dance 'The Mess'. You jus' keep your feet together and move your bowels.

ANTONIO: Sire, you must try t' obey the rules o' the 'Pavan'. The steps 're decreed and not subject t' impulses o' the moment.

CARLOS: KINGS aaaaren't subject t' rules, decrees, *French* decrees! I watch you *close*, Master Antonio, you flirt wi' TREASON wi' your French words, French ribbons, French perfumes.

ANTONIO: But my *feet* are Spanish, Your Majesty.

CARLOS: They look suspiciously French t' meeee. Mean-minded feet, little sodomitic feet. (ANTONIO *tries to hide them.*) And the *toes* whaa o' the toes?!

ANTONIO: They're loyal, Sire, all ten o' 'em!

CARLOS: I dance f' joy na-aaa i' thy cold French way.

ANTONIO: 'Tis manifi . . . 'er, magnificent, Your Majesty, but,
  'er 'tisn't the 'Pavan'.
CARLOS: No, 'tis 'The Carlos'!

A drum roll. They line up opposite the mirrors: CARLOS, ALBA
and TORRES *on one side:* RAFAEL *and* MONTERREY *on the other.*
ANTONIO *poses between them Stage Centre. He raps three times
with his staff. The mirrors bevel and* ANA *and* FOUR LADIES-IN-
WAITING *step out from behind them and take their places beside
the men.*

*They make reverence. Drum, viol and lute play 'Belle Que Tient
Ma Vie' and they dance Down Stage following* CARLOS's *grotesque
jerkings exactly.*

With their MAJESTIES *in the lead, they wobble, lurch, do the
splits, skid and spin with poker-faced dignity. Only* ANTONIO
*tries to do the stately 'Pavan', but as they reverse and dance back
Up Stage, he succumbs and joins the* OTHERS *in their grotesque
cavortings. The music grows faster, until the climax is reached with
the male dancers all simultaneously keeling over onto the floor with
a crash.*

Blackout, amid delighted laughter, congratulations and applause.

SCENE V

Spot up Down Stage Right on MARIANA *praying.*

MARIANA: Lord God, let my son live and his son live as Thy
  Son lives, eternally. Nail my thoughts t' Thy Cross as Thy
  Son's hands and feet were nailed. I'm in the forge, under the
  hammer. I pray, let Carlos live! (*She thrusts out her neck and
  speaks in a hysterical parrot-like croak.*) *But he's half-dead, clod
  back t' clod, his child'll die, I'd six die so why shouldst his live if
  mine died, go stink and die CRRAH CRRAH.* Sweet Jesus, Holy
  Son save him f' we're as dust, *and in my youth I ruled the Spanish
  Empire as Regent. Authority's the only air I can breathe.*

  B—2*

*I'll sign this—this—this—this. Now I gasp and count grains o'
sand, let the donkey-dick stink and die, let me breathe again, Joey's
a good boy. CRRAH CRRAH.* Holy Virgin Mother, I see dead
goiters skewered on spits, 'tis one o' the 144,000 torments o'
Hell *which I embrace gladly if my chicken-hammed son and family'd
die, Hell holds no surprises, I'm staked out daily, pain like as a
wedge, air slashed wi' knives dat's a good boy, Joey.* But he's my
flesh. I bore him *and he bores me, CRRAH. CRRAH.* Oh Lord,
my life's full o' sorrow, *here today gone tomorrow.* God's the
answer, *what's the question? CRRAH. CRRAH.* I ask, I sweat,
I wonder. I swallow the world i' a yawn. (*Gasping asthmatically.*)
Aiai . . . Aiai . . . Aiai. . . . (*Violently.*) *GRRRRX CRRAH
CRRAH.* . . .

*Jamming the Bible into her mouth she flaps her arms desperately
as her Spot goes out to the sound of singing.*

SCENE VI

TWO WOMEN *are singing a German nursery rhyme:* 'Schlaf,
Kinderl, schlaf!/ Der Vater hüt die schaf,/ de Mutter schüttelt's
Bäumelein,/ de fällt herab en Träumelein,/ Schlaf, Kinderl,
schlaf!' *as lights Up Stage Right and Left on wall panel—the
reverse sides of the mirrors—showing tranquil scenes from the Nativity with the Virgin and Child.*

Then lights full up on the Queen's private room to show ANA, *Stage
Left with her companion, the stumpy,* CONDESA BELEPSCH
*happily cataloguing piles of 'objets d'art' stacked on the table and
overflowing chests on the floor. There is a smaller table nearby with
bowls of spiced cucumbers and next to it the* PARROT *on its perch.
Doors Up Stage Centre.*

ANA *picks up various items whilst* BELEPSCH *ticks them off in a ledger.*

ANA: One crystal orb, set wi' emeralds and diamonds, surmounted by a cross o' gold; one rosary o' oriental pearls; one

spherical clock-watch circa 1550; Gifts taken from the Conde
de Harrach and t' be sent t' my brother John, along wi' the
tapestry, armchairs, mahogany chest and the ten Ruben
landscapes . . . (*Eating cucumbers.*) Seventeen brothers and
sisters spawning across Europe and all expecting me t' enrich
'em.

BELEPSCH: The grandees fear your visits more than those o' the
Inquisitor-General himself.

ANA: Mama said 'Those who ask shan't have, those who don't
ask won't get'. So I take. I smile, I frown, I squeeze. Our
Spanish lords deserve t' be gutted o' their surplus gold and
silver—sneezing at me i' the shadows, jeering behind corners!
(*Patting stomach.*) But my power grows wi' my belly. My
happiness too; when the Queen Mother's finally banished
'twill be complete.

PARROT: *Cock-bawd. Crrah. Crrah.*

ANA: And my people'll love me. I'll hold up my son and they'll
shout, 'God Save the Queen! God Save the Queen'.

BELEPSCH: Ihre Majestät es war ein schweres Exil.

ANA: 'Tas been hard from the night we landed at Corona, when
I saw my kingly bridegroom f' the first time and I wanted t'
go back home. His sores sickened me, decay stank from his
fingers, spittle filled his kisses, lice jumped from 'tween his
hollow thighs. I'm Queen o' a cold land. Alone 'cept f' you
dear Condesa and my Joey.

PARROT: *Joey's a darlin' boy, a darlin' boy.*

BELEPSCH: Cling t'our friendship, sweet dove, 'tis our rock . . .
and the childhood we shared together i' the Old Country.
(*Singing low.*) 'Schlaf, Kinderl, schlaf' . . .

ANA
BELEPSCH } (*singing*): 'Dein Vater ist ein Graf,/dein Mutter is
eine Bauerndirn/soll ihr Kinderl selber wiegn/Schlaf, Kinderl,
schlaf.'

There is a knock on the door. BELEPSCH *crosses and opens it
and* ALMIRANTE *and* MOTILLA *enter bowing.*

BELEPSCH: Your Majesty, the Almirante de Castilla and Father Motilla.

ANA: Didst she turn pale?! Didst she bite her lip till 't bled?!

MOTILLA: When I told her o' your condition, the Queen Mother was struck dumb.

ANA: *Ahhhhh* . . . Soon her silence'll be e'erlasting. She's t' be exiled t' the Convent o' the Sisters o' Mercy.

> The PARROT *screeches mockingly.* ANA, BELEPSCH *and* ALMIRANTE *smile.*

MOTILLA: Vengeance is mine, sayeth the Lord. Hate the sin, love the sinner. Though I find His Eminence the Cardinal-Archbishop Pontocarrero personally repugnant—he wears silk 'gainst the skin—'tis his sins I damn. He tolerates Protestant heretics abroad and iniquities at home.

ALMIRANTE: F' Lent he's giving up penances. I once asked him what a priest was. He said he was a man too lazy t' work and too frightened t' steal.

MOTILLA: No. A priest is a man good as grass, better than bread. But thanks t'His Eminence, ours hunt, dice, dance and lie; so greed and lechery flourish.

PARROT: *Lechery, lechery.*

ANA: I see little lechery, Father. Spaniards only become stiff wi' pride.

MOTILLA: Lechery's everywhere child; eyes, ears, smell, touch, taste, all senses tempt us t' it f' man's a monstrous centaur, a war 'tween his extremities. A priest fights t' keep God afore his eyes. He walks only wi' angels. His Eminence talks only wi' men.

ALMIRANTE: I envy you your enemy, Father. Now our faction's triumphed, Your Majesty, gi' me leave to' rejoin my command.

ANA: You shared our defeats, dear Almirante, now share our victory; we need you wi' us always.

MOTILLA: We need only God, from whence all succour flows.

ANA: And love flows too, Father. F' God answered my night
cries and came t' me i' the falling sickness. He came and St
Brigitta unclenched my teeth, St Augustine undid my belt,
St Catherine lifted my dress, St Francis stepped aside, I was
enrapped, flung down, forced open, swallowed up as he thrust
a gold spear into my heart and the fire was a soft caress. Conceived in such ecstasy my babe'll be as beautiful as the Christ
child. I dream o' his baptism . . . (*Lights down slightly*, *Down
Stage*.) The grandees, Princes and great ladies o' Spain waiting
in the Royal Chapel . . . The choir singing 'Gloria in Excelsis.'
. . . (*A choir sings softly but the words cannot be heard*.) Our royal
nurse, Dona Maria Engracia de Toledo Marquesa de los Veleze
carrying in my son. . . .

She smiles at the vision as the MARQUESA *enters haughtily
Wings Left in white, with the baby in white christening robes in
her arms. She crosses Down Stage Centre.*

MOTILLA: The ceremony must be performed by Don Sebastien
Vega, Patriarch o' the Indies. He's too old, but etiquette
demands 't.

ANA *nods and the aged Patriarch in white mitre and stole staggers
in Wings Right carrying a font and altar ladle and crosses Stage
Centre. He stops, exhausted, opposite the* NURSE *and* CHILD *and
places the font between them.*

ALMIRANTE: 'Twill be a glorious moment when he recites the
Credo. 'Credis in Deum Patrem omnipotem Creatorum coeli
et terrae?'

ANA: Credo. . . ! Credo. . . ! Credo. . . ! and he'll take my son
(*the* PATRIARCH *takes the* BABY) saying t' the Godfathers
'NAME THIS CHILD', and they'll name him and he'll make the
sign o' the Cross and pour sweet Jordan water o'er his head
(*the* PATRIARCH *dips the ladle into the font*) saying, saying,
saying . . . Carlos, John, Philip, Sebastien, Egmont I BAPTIZE
THEE IN THE NAME O' THE . . . *urg*.

As she steps forward excitedly Down Stage the PATRIARCH
turns and flings the contents of the ladle at her; her face and apron

are drenched in blood. The PARROT *screeches but the* OTHERS *behind her are unaware of anything being wrong.*

ANA *is transfixed as the* PATRIARCH *pours blood over the* BABY *and exits backwards with it Wings Right whilst the* MARQUESA *exits similarly with the font, Wings Left.*

ANA (*softly*): Dreams liquefy . . . limbs fall . . . soft lumps float past . . . hand feet finger eye pink mouth lattice veins dead meat slimed away . . . O sweet Mary, Mother o' Mercy craters spurt i' my belly . . . cauterize 't wi' hot irons vises winches ropes gibbets . . . words rot . . . There's no Indies, no font, choir, baptism, *child*!

MOTILLA: No baptism? No child? Why?

ANA: I BLEED.

PARROT: *Jesus saves but Moses invests. Crrah Crrah.*

BELEPSCH: Du lieber Gott!

She crosses quickly and escorts ANA *to a chair.* MOTILLA *and* ALMIRANTE *are stunned.*

ANA: He's drowned in blood. I'm washed empty.

ALMIRANTE: But all the signs confirmed Your Majesties'd achieved a perfect conception.

ANA: Immaculate rather than perfect. I know the signs better than my owl-blind astrologers and physicians. *I bleed.*

ALMIRANTE: The wheel spins.

MOTILLA: And we're abject underfoot.

ALMIRANTE: We feel thy loss, Your Majesty.

MOTILLA: And Spain'll hate thee f' 't.

BELEPSCH *has removed the bloody apron as* ANA *wipes her face. It is now chalk white.*

ANA: Hatred's the air we breathe. Nothing's changed. Reality's no obstacle. 'Twill be four weeks afore Dr Bravo's allowed t' examine me again. Time enough t' defeat our enemies and make Charles o' Austria heir.

They all look at each other.

MOTILLA (*slowly*): Naturally Your Majesty must wait f' Dr Bravo t' reveal the truth. For 'twill not be acknowledged such till he reveals 't. Once only priests were the universal truth-bearers, now 'tis the coming men o' science. I pray in the four weeks afore he pronounces judgement, God may reverse His, and staunch the wound, f' He e'er watches o'er us in His mercy.

ANA: So doeth the Queen Mother, wi'out any. So *we* must watch ourselves, watch ourselves . . . I tire, gentlemen. You may withdraw.

MOTILLA *and* ALMIRANTE *bow and exit Up Stage Centre.*

BELEPSCH: Weep now, my lady.

ANA: Tears'd be noted and held against me. My heart daren't break, she'd see 't breaking. I can only smile and smile and smile and smile and smile AND . . . (*Singing a snatch to herself she takes up exactly the same position as at the beginning of the scene Stage Right.*) 'Schlaf, kinderl, Schlaf/Der Tod sitzt auf der Stange . . .' (*Lights down to a Spot on her as she resumes cataloguing.*) Gifts taken from the Corregidor Don Francisco de Vasco: one onyx scarabeus; one gold ring wi' a cluster o' . . . (*She frowns, whips out a jeweller's eye-glass, screws it into her eye and peers closely.*) Paste! Another Ananias! Cheat! Cheat! Five plates painted wi' the marriage o' Cupid and Psyche; two crucifixes, gold; (*The eyeglass drops from her eye.*) She'll ne'er find out. How could she if I smile and smile? . . . one baby's rattle, ivory . . . Smile. I'll learn t' smile . . . Six Nuremberg dolls: St Cecilia wi' musical instruments, St Theodoras wi' armour, St Florian wi' buckets, St Peter wi' keys, St John wi' lamb, St Christopher wi' child!

As faint white vapour envelops her and the Spot fades out, another woman's voice, also reeling off a list of items, mingles with hers.

SCENE VII

Spot up through steamy vapour Down Stage Right on a mountain of dirty clothes. Straddled on top of it is the Head Washerwoman, THERESA DIEGO, *in a leather apron and clogs.* MARIANA *watches her impatiently from below as she picks up each item of dirty washing, sniffs it to identify the stains and throws it down into a large basket near the foot of the ladder leaning against the pile.*

THERESA: Property o' Her Catholic Majesty Queen Ana, one satin petticoat, stained wi' sweat and tallow grease. Two shifts, spotted wi' powder and aged sweet-water . . . Property o' His Most Catholic Majesty; one vest encrusted in week-old vomit and dribble . . . Property o' Her Majesty Queen Ana, four pairs o' stockings soiled wi' Madrid mud. One lace saberqua peppered wi' holy water . . .

MARIANA: *Blood.* Doest she bleed? I suspect she's bleeding. Only tell me if she's bleeding. Doest smell blood?

THERESA: Ne'er fear, if she's pinked I'll smell 't out, Ma'am. Even after twenty years as Head Washerwoman t' the Royal House most stains still look much alike. Who canst tell the difference twixt red wine, plum jam, ochre or blood? Cow or donkey dung? Peepers is deceived but not this snout. (*Taps nose.*) Once I've smelt out the blot it can be washed, rubbed, salted or vinegared away according. My fame's up me nostrils, Ma'am, they've ne'er failed me. 'Tis a blessed gift. Now I's oft called on t' sniff out the Devil. Holy work, holy work! He cometh in many shapes but always wi' the same Devil's stench straight from the great privee o' Hell. 'Tis a yellow, greenish, many-layered stink-o. I ne'er mistake it, Ma'am. I'm sniffing my way to Salvation! (*She takes out a small box and sniffs snuff loudly.*) Must keep the snot-passages clear, they're most tender. (*She dabs her nose delicately with a handkerchief and resumes sniffing the laundry;* MARIANA *ignores her and says her beads.*) I still recall the first time I sniffed His Majesty's dirt-stained drawers. I've ne'er had a moment's sickness since, though I coffined three clapped-out husbands. The King's touch cures all distempers and His Majesty's healing powers still cling t' his filthy linen. By the blessed nose o' the Abbess Eba, odours is revealing, Ma'am. I can predicate the future by smell better than all yer

star-men wi' their Jupiters and Mercurys. When royal shirts
're soiled wi' wine and feasting, 't means good times ahead,
but if they reek o' incense and holy water then trouble comes
apace. 'Tis all in 'Mother Diego's Odour Almanack: The
Future Prophetical Deduced from Royal Linen' . . . Your
Eminence! Father Froylan . . .!

She falls on her knees as PONTOCARRERO *enters Stage Left*
with FATHER FROYLAN, *complete with his pouch of State papers.*

PONTOCARRERO: Ma'am, the Royal Washhouse's no place f' a
Queen Mother.

FROYLAN: This heat's a foretaste o' Hell.

MARIANA: 'Tis my home till I find proof against her. You desert
my cause, Eminence.

PONTOCARRERO: My only cause is Spain, her throne and
Empire. A Spanish heir'll save both.

MARIANA: She lies. She bleeds and lies.

PONTOCARRERO: The Queen may lie but not Father Motilla,
I'm certain, e'en though I find his person repugnant.

FROYLAN: They say he weareth *two* hairshirts.

PONTOCARRERO: Dominicans 're so ostentatious i' their dress.
He practises all the austerities o' his Order, except the most
beneficial—perpetual silence.

FROYLAN: I've never liked him and I always will.

PONTOCARRERO: Saints're a blessing in heaven but hell on
earth. He's fallen into the heresy o' confusing religion wi'
ethics. But he's not a man t' lie.

MARIANA: Not knowingly.

PONTOCARRERO: But what o' the physicians who confirm the
pregnancy?

MARIANA: For the first two months in practice every physician
wants t' save humanity; after that they only want t' save
money. (*To* THERESA.) Why art kneeling, woman? Sniff!

THERESA: It's too full o' awe, Ma'am. To be honoured by Your
Highness and the Cardinal Archbishop in one day. This
Washhouse'll become a shrine. Gi' 't blessing, Your Eminence.

Deep in thought, PONTOCARRERO *makes the sign of the Cross and mumbles a blessing.*

FROYLAN: Ma'am, you're in the hands o' the best nose in Spain. I've had occasion t' use Signora Diego's snout t' sniff out Lucifer's minions. Demonology's my particular hobby.

MARIANA: Sniff! Sniff!

THERESA *rises and resumes searching whilst* PONTOCARRERO *strokes his beard thoughtfully.*

FROYLAN: Why didn't you get more help, Ma'am? At my last accounting the Royal Washhouse employed some twenty-three haulers, forty washers, thirty-six dryers and eighteen young scrubbers.

MARIANA: They all've mouths and walls've ears. If the Queen knew we were searching she'd hide her guilty drawers and petticoats. Faster, woman! Faster!

PONTOCARRERO: Father, go help the woman.

FROYLAN: But Eminence, 'tisn't meet. I've despatches, warrants, documents t' draft. (*Indicates his stuffed pouch.*) The wheels o' State turn on paper.

PONTOCARRERO: When you entered the Society o' Jesus, thy fourth vow as a Jesuit was t' go wi'out question or delay wherever you might be ordered f' the salvation o' souls. (*He gestures to the pile.*) Go, my son.

FROYLAN: Forgive me, Eminence.

He nervously starts climbing up the ladder.

PONTOCARRERO: Ma'am, I believe the Queen's pregnant. But 'tis possible hope clouds judgement.

Groaning to himself FROYLAN *reaches the top of the pile.* THERESA *kisses his hand and he looks nervously down at* PONTOCARRERO *and* MARIANA. *They continue talking as* FROYLAN *whispers inquiringly to* THERESA.

MARIANA: She'll've no children. She's BLOCKED like her predecessor, now and forever.

PONTOCARRERO: You forget the efficacy o' prayer, the soul's breath. A million voices rise up daily: 'Make their Majesties fertile.' As our sins brought forth their sterility, so our prayers brought forth . . .

FROYLAN: Blood?!

PONTOCARRERO: } *Where? Where?*
MARIANA:

FROYLAN: Why're we looking f' blood, Your Eminence? Who's dead?

MARIANA: We are if thou doesn't find any.

THERESA: 'Tis blood from the miraculous pitcher which holds water wi' its mouth downwards; from her quim, her doodle sack.

FROYLAN *is still bewildered but starts examining the dirty clothes with obvious distaste. But this soon changes to sly pleasure as he fondles petticoats and drawers.*

MARIANA: Ah, the efficacy o' prayer! But still my son's jaw juts so his teeth casn't meet, and he swallows chicken gizzards whole, afore voiding 'em back up again. Some days he canst hardly stand upright. Yet our iron wills beat and break against his weakness.

PONTOCARRERO: His weakness has saved Spain.

MARIANA: Only wi' my help. But now he preens and struts about the stage, cocksure at last. He plans t' banish me.

PONTOCARRERO: How d'you know?

MARIANA: I can see through walls.

FROYLAN (*excitedly waving drawers*): I've found 't . . .! Stains, blood . . . *Ahhhhhhhhhh.*

As he rushes across to show THERESA *the centre of the pile suddenly collapses and he disappears down the hole.*

THERESA: Father Froylan!

MARIANA: The stains, the stains! Don't lose the stains!

She starts climbing up the ladder followed by PONTOCARRERO *whilst* THERESA *leans over the hole.*

FROYLAN (*off*): Help . . . I'm choking . . . the stench . . .

THERESA *grabs the unseen* FROYLAN *and pulls him up. His flushed face finally appears over the edge of the hole.*

THERESA: N-e-a-r-l-y there Fa . . . Ma'am!

FROYLAN: *Ahhhhhhhh.*

Awe-struck at the sight of MARIANA *and* PONTOCARRERO *clambering up beside her,* THERESA *has let go of* FROYLAN *who falls back down the hole.* THERESA *flops on to her knees.*

THERESA: Your Highness, Your Eminence, here on top o' my pile. The honour . . . the glory . . .

MARIANA: The blood?!

PONTOCARRERO (*calling down the hole*): Stop playing the fool, Father, nations are at risk. No time f' cap and bells.

FROYLAN (*off*): Help . . . help . . .

PONTOCARRERO and THERESA *lean over the hole and heave* FROYLAN *up by his shoulders.*

PONTOCARRERO: Where's the bloody garment?

FROYLAN: I dropped 't afore I fell . . . *Ahhhhhhhh.*

PONTOCARRERO and THERESA *have let go of* FROYLAN *and he disappears yet again as they frantically search.* MARIANA *pounces on a petticoat.*

MARIANA: Stains! Is't proof, woman? Is't? Is't?

THERESA takes the garment and sniffs a stain.

THERESA: Red wine, Ma'am . . . (*Sniffs.*) Burgundy. A Musigny '32. Inferior vintage.

MARIANA: 'Tis here, I know 't.

PONTOCARRERO (*looking down the hole*): Father, don't jus' lie there using up air.

FROYLAN (*groaning*): *Ahhh. Ahhh.*

PONTOCARRERO: What? Oh, nonsense!

THERESA: Ne'er fear, Ma'am, this nose's pledged t' serve thee t' the last sniff.

MARIANA: Quicker, rattle-pate, quicker. Sniff, sniff. Sniff everybody, sniff!

As they sniff and search frantically, FOUR HOODED MONKS *enter Wings Right.*

Chanting 'Hallelujah Brothers' they drag off the pile, Wings Left, singing solemnly.

MONKS ⎫
THERESA ⎬ (singing): 'Sniff, Brothers, Sniff; Sniff, Brothers,
⎭ Sniff. Sniff, Brothers, Sniff Brothers, Sniff Sniff Sniff Sniff. You gotta see the light/ You gotta pull your load/ You gotta help the cause/ You gotta smell the clothes/ You gotta pitch right in or hit the road/ Then Sniff Sniff Sniff Sniff Sniff./ You gotta find the costume/ You gotta spot the gear/ You gotta scent the tiger/ You gotta smell the smear/ You gotta see your dentist twice a year./ And Sniff Sniff Sniff Sniff Sniff/ Sniff Brothers Sniff, Sniff Brothers Sniff, Sniff Brothers Sniff, Brothers, Sniff Sniff Sniff Sniff Sniff.'

SCENE VIII

As the pile disappears there is a fanfare of trumpets and dim lights come up.

Large objects covered with white dust-sheets loom out of the surrounding white vapour and the ghostly bare-headed figures of MONTERREY, ALMIRANTE, TORRES *and* ALBA *face* CARLOS *who stands bolt upright, tall and imposing Down Stage Left, the Golden Fleece insignia glittering round his neck. He is flanked by* DR BRAVO *and the* COURT ASTROLOGER, HERMONYMOUS GONGORA, *a beaky old man with a zodiac pendant and conical hat. Bare-headed, and on one knee in front of them is the French Ambassador* PIERRE REBENAC.

TWO PRIESTS *in white robes and swinging thuribles of incense remove the dust sheets to reveal large children's toys: a rocking horse, alphabet bricks, drum and cradle.* A THIRD PRIEST *blesses them with lustral water from a stoup whilst voices echo with metallic harshness.*

DR BRAVO (*intoning*): We declare Her Most Catholic Majesty's in a state o' being wi' child, her delivery will take place i' the allotted time, if God so wills and no foul vapours invade her uterus. *Foul vapours begone.*

GONGORA (*intoning*): We declare Her Most Catholic Majesty
'll enter a most fruitful period wi' Mercury and Saturn i' the
angle of the 10th Royal House and Aquarius ascending t' the
horizon o' the Spanish Court, if God so wills and no malicious
aspects cross her House o' Life. *Malicious aspects begone.*

CARLOS: Monsieur Rebenac, go tell thy master Louis thou
hast seen the royal nursery consecrated t' receive Spain's
future king. If thy armies move against us, all Christendom'll
know your sovereign fights to usurp a legimate heir.

Rhythmic clapping from the Court. CARLOS *leans forward stiffly
and touches the Ambassador's hat.* REBENAC *puts it on before
speaking, according to etiquette. The rest of the Court follow
suit.*

REBENAC: Sire, my Most Catholic Majesty, Louis o' France,
shares the joy o' this pregnancy. 'Tis my belief, all division
'twixt nations canst be overcome by diplomacy. In this I speak
f' France . . .

CARLOS: But I do not speak f' Spain. I *am* Spain.

CARLOS *touches his own hat. The audience is over. A fanfare
of trumpets.* REBENAC *and the others withdraw, bowing.*

One of the PRIESTS *lifts* CARLOS's *cloak and removes a long,
flat, wooden board which has been clamped to his back to keep him
upright, whilst* ANOTHER *takes off wooden platforms strapped to
his shoes. They then exit, Wings Right and Left.*

*Lights full up on the Royal Nursery. The walls are covered with
blue drapes and there are* TWO ATTENDANTS *on the doors Up
Stage Centre.*

Alone, CARLOS *is back to normal, his limbs jerk continuously as
he stumbles around happily, setting the wooden horse rocking.*

CARLOS: III aaaaam Spain. Now I canst make a noise wi' my
feet, must grip my mind. (*He grabs the wooden horse and stops
it rocking.*) Grip. Grip. Grip.

Bubbles float out of the cradle. RAFAEL *jumps out blowing soap
bubbles.*

RAFAEL (*singing*): 'As I was going t' sell my eggs, I meet a man wi' bandy legs. Bandy legs and crooked toes. I tripped up his heels and he fell on his nose.'

CARLOS: Didst see? Didst see meeee gi' audience? I didst not fall down once, nor vomit up, nor piss my breeches, nor rap out a stinkin' volley. I CRUSHED Monsieur Reverence aaaaas I'll crush his Master.

RAFAEL: 'Twas proudly done, Sire. Diplomats are like as crabs and women; seeming t' come they go; seeming t' go they come.

CARLOS: I'm gripping my mind. I must aaaaaapoint a First Minister. Whoooo's worthy, Tom?

RAFAEL: Appoint a man o' the lower sort, Sire, wi'out pedigree or land. He'd've t' look only t' you f' advancement.

CARLOS: You're Jo-Jo-Josephusing again. Whaaaa o' my grandees and clergy?

RAFAEL: Chain the clergy t' their altars and imprison the grandees deeper in etiquette. (*He takes out a small brush and sweeps the ground whilst bowing.*) And reward 'em wi' bigger ribbons and titles. (*He puts a large rosette to his chest.*) Being men they prefer the shadow t' the substance, pleased t' crouch, they'll be eager t' crawl.

CARLOS: Thou art aaaa funny little ffffellow. Hast always been soooo small?

RAFAEL: No Sire, I've been ill.

CARLOS: *Honk honk.* . . Illness made mmme dwarfish too. My nursery was a sickbed. I'd no time t' play. Whaaa games do children play?

RAFAEL (*counting*): 'Inter mitzy, bitzy tool/ Ira dira dominu/ Oker poker dominoker/ Out goes YOU.' That's one I played when I was small. And blind man's buff; frog i' the middle; puss i' the corner; Jack, Jack, shine a light; fathers and mothers; stampers. . . .

CARLOS: Stampers? Whaaaa . . .?

RAFAEL: 'Twas to see who couldst stamp on the other's toes, Sire.

Grinning, CARLOS *stumbles forward trying to stamp on* RAFAEL'*s toes. But the dwarf darts away pursued by* CARLOS *laughing idiotically. The chase continues round the toys till at last* RAFAEL *climbs up on the bricks.*

Still laughing CARLOS *lurches over to the* ATTENDANTS *by the door, and stamps triumphantly on their toes crying 'Stampers!'. No reaction from them whatsoever.*

CARLOS *comes back to* RAFAEL, *delighted.*

CARLOS: We'll command my lord Alba t' play wi' us.

RAFAEL: When I want t' play with a prick, I'll play with my own.

ATTENDANTS: *Ahhhhh.*

As the ATTENDANTS *hop about yelling in pain there is a loud knock and the doors Up Stage Centre open to reveal* ANA *and* MARIANA *accompanied by* MOTILLA *and* PONTOCARRERO *respectively.*

They advance quickly, ignoring each other, then suddenly stop and stare in amazement at the frenetic antics of the ATTENDANTS *as they hop back to their places.*

CARLOS (*low*): TThey've come t' tear the skin fffffrom my soul. Tom, Tom, I'm the world's oldest living orphan.

RAFAEL (*low*): Don't give 'em permission t' speak, Sire. They're not allowed t' speak until you speak.

1ST ATTENDANT: Sire, Her Most Catholic Majesty, Queen Ana o' Spain.

2ND ATTENDANT: Sire, Her Royal Highness, the Queen Mother.

The women rush Downstage, each wanting to get to CARLOS *first. They curtsey in front of him, he nods, they rise and wait for him to speak. Instead he stares past them.* ANA *frowns, opens her mouth to say something but* MOTILLA *gestures for her to be silent. Impatiently* MARIANA *steps forward to speak but* PONTO-CARRERO *shakes his head.*

The silence becomes oppressive.

Finally they explode in wordless fury. MARIANA *jabs an accusing finger towards* ANA *who bites the air in rage.* MARIANA

then breaks an invisible bar across her knee with a 'crack' whilst
ANA *makes vicious tearing gestures.* MARIANA *wrings an imagi-*
nary neck whilst ANA *mimes gouging out an eye. Uttering thin*
screeching sounds, MARIANA *grinds her heel as* ANA *claws the air*
sobbing with rage.

    CARLOS *gasps and clutches his throat, trembling.*

CARLOS: I cccchoke . . .

ANA: *Lying slush-bucket.*

MARIANA: *Hedge-whore.*

ANA: Carlos, thou swore she'd be banished.

CARLOS: Maaaamaaaa.

MARIANA: Carlos, thou swore she'd be curbed.

CARLOS: Anaaaaa you poison my unborn child's mind against
me.

ANA: How?

CARLOS: By writing fffffoul notes about meee and swallowing
'em. Dat's mind poisoning AND there's air poisoning,
loneliness-poisoning, weakness-poisoning, too-much-reading
poisoning, repeated-coitus-poisoning, XX-poisoning . . .

ANA: And foetus-poisoning. She mixes Jambala flowers i' cow's
urine turning my womb into cold rice gruel. Our child'll be a
deformed CRETIN!

CARLOS: *Ahh. Ahh. I'll banish her.*

    He jerks across to MOTILLA *who is ready with a document and*
portable quill and ink.

PONTOCARRERO: Sire, 'tis mere superstition. Everything God
makes is perfect.

RAFAEL: What about me?

PONTOCARRERO: Why, you're the most perfect cross-eyed
dwarf I've ever seen.

ANA: O-U-T spells 'out'. She goes OUT.

RAFAEL (*pointing to* MARIANA): She means you.

CARLOS: Maaaaamaa t' save our child.

MARIANA: Her womb's as empty as her heart.

ANA: Old lies, old woman!

MARIANA (*triumphantly*): Here's new proof then! (*She holds up blood-stained pair of women's drawers.*) Blood. *Thy blood.*

CARLOS: Whaaaa . . .?

MARIANA: The clock strikes, you stream; this drop condemns thee and this half drop pulls thee down. *Guilty.*

ANA: Show 't me, show 't me.

She grabs the garment but MARIANA *won't let go. As they tug,* PONTOCARRERO *quickly helps* MARIANA *and* MOTILLA, ANA. RAFAEL *encourages them.*

Gibbering with frustration CARLOS *unsheathes his sword and with a wild, lucky swipe slashes the garment in two. The teams fall back.*

CARLOS: Whaaa . . .?

MOTILLA: Christ bleeds f' man's redemption, women f' his iniquities.

PONTOCARRERO: If a woman bleeds from the notch, Sire, t's a certain sign she doeth not conceive.

MARIANA: See here the Queen's own crest, gold and purple. Dare she deny 'tis hers, son. In front o' thy Sovereign Lord and thy Confessor, deny 't, Madam.

ANA: The garment's mine.

MARIANA: *Crrah. Crrah.*

CARLOS (*falling on his knees and beating the toy drum*): Poor peee poor peee eee.

ANA: The garment's mine but not the blood. 'Tis rat's blood, bat's blood, cat's blood, not my blood.

CARLOS *stops beating the drum.*

PONTOCARRERO: Come, Your Majesty, 'twas found in my presence i' the Royal Washhouse.

ANA: Where she'd placed it f' thee t' find, first having stolen and smear'd 't. O she's a cunning lady. By the blood o' our Saviour, 'tis true. Jus' look at her Judas face.

PONTOCARRERO *and the* OTHERS *look at* MARIANA.

MARIANA: Lent-breaker, the physician'll confirm who's Judas-faced when he examines thee i' the morning.

ANA: He'll examine me four weeks hence according t' etiquette and not afore, else all Europe'll know the Queen's condition's doubted.

MOTILLA: And then the country'd be plunged back into factions clamouring f' the Bavarian José, the Austrian Charles and the French Philip.

ANA: Do I not suffer enough? Already I've dog-headed, web-fingered nightmares. Wilt our child be whole? What diseases 'll run through his veins? Wilt his swaddling clothes be his winding sheet? I need peace o' mind at this time and mountains o' gooseberry fool. Wi' thy permission, Sire, I'll wi'draw and leave your mother t' her hatchings!

Flinging her torn piece of cloth at MARIANA*'s feet, she curtseys and as* CARLOS *offers her his arm to the door, sweeps Up Stage with him and exits, followed by* MOTILLA.

The OTHERS *watch in silence as* CARLOS *gazes after her.*

RAFAEL: I think I'll go where the climate suits my clothes.

CARLOS: Sssssshe carest only f' peace o' mind and gooseberry fool. Maaaaamaaaa if thou carest f' meeee, CARE f' her now.

MARIANA: If I care? When you were born physicians whispered 'Ma'am, his body's rotten as a pear, 'tisn't in our power t' save him long.' But I did penance, winding barbed rope round my waist, fasted and prayed daily: Our Lady've mercy . . . Our Lady've mercy . . . Our Lady've mercy . . . Our Lady've mercy . . . she lies . . . (*Gasping.*) Let me breathe . . . Mama knows best . . .

CARLOS: Maamaaa.

MARIANA: *Crrah . . . Crrah . . . Crrah.*

PONTOCARRERO *bows and guides* MARIANA *out Up Stage Centre, gasping and cawing plaintively whilst* CARLOS *staggers into the cradle Down Stage Right crying* 'Maamaaa'.

RAFAEL *sighs, takes a drink from a tiny hip-flask and crosses to* CARLOS *curled up in the cradle. Lights down to a Spot as* RAFAEL *rocks him gently.*

RAFAEL (*singing*): 'I had a little nut tree. Nothing would 't bear./ But a silver nutmeg. And a golden pear./The King o' Spain's daughter came to visit me./And all for the sake o' my little nut tree.'

Spot out to the sound of whipping.

SCENE IX

Spot up Stage Left to show MOTILLA, *stripped to the waist, kneeling under a crucifix hanging horizontally from the Flies, and being whipped by a hooded Dominican* MONK.

MOTILLA: Lord have mercy according to thy loving kindness. Look upon my humility and pain. Let not mine enemies triumph. (*To* MONK.) *Harder, harder, lay on, lay on* . . . Our cause's just. We'll send forth our priests, barefoot, t' preach the word and help the poor. F' they casn't wi'stand the rich who covet their fields and seize 'em by violence. Help me Lord now, when all seems lost. Show me thy angelic will, illumine my eyes, tell me what I must do. Grant me a vision. (*To* MONK.) *Lay on, I say. Harder. Where didst you learn t' flagellate? Thou hasn't even drawn blood yet.* Make this cell a furnace, in Babylon where the three men found the Son o' God, make it a burning bush, a pillar o' cloud speaking unto Moses: speak t' me, Lord! (*To* MONK.) *Lay on, spider-shanks. Put your back into 't.* Grant me a vision, Lord . . . *lay on harder,* a vision . . . harder . . . a vision . . . vis . . . har . . . vis . . . har . . . vis . . . v i . . 'vvvvvvv . . . a vision.

The MONK *falls back exhausted as a vertical beam of light strikes a couch Stage Right where* ALMIRANTE *is making love to two half-naked* WOMEN.

MOTILLA (*making the sign of the Cross*): Adjúro ergo te omnis immundissime spiritus, omne phantásma omnis incúrsio sátanae in nómine Jesus Christi Nazaréni. You come again t' tempt me, Lucifer. But 'tis a temptation f' this pea-green novice, not a scarred veteran o' Christ! You know well I've slain lust, burnt out lechery. I see those two lumps o' lace-mutton carrion fluttering their legs afore me, already skull-bald, grave-yard dead and stinkin'. Lucifer, return and take thy puny visions wi' thee! (*Nothing happens, he closes his eyes and concentrates.*) I command thee in the name o' Christ Our Saviour, BEGONE.

He opens his eyes but the vision remains. Naked bodies, frenzied caresses and voices: 'My darling! My darling!'

As they reach a climax of love-making, three glowing haloes drop from the Flies and hang over their heads. MOTILLA *stares in disbelief.*

MOTILLA (*slowly*): Then 'tis Thy vision, Lord, not Lucifer's. (*A choir sings softly.*) Yes, now I see 't all plain . . . Jesu, Jesu, break, crush, humble, hollow and fill me wi' Thy holy spirit that whilst shovelling shit I'll not stink!

The MONK *is about to start whipping again but* MOTILLA *gestures curtly and is handed a towel. As he briskly wipes himself down and is helped with his habit, lights come up slowly.*

MOTILLA: Ten minutes o' flagellation a day's a tonic; the key t' inner health. Remember, a limp-wrist 's a sign o' weakness— if not worse. 'Tis our nature t' inflict pain. But cruelty cannot run free, like crude ore 't must be refined in the service o' Jesus Christ. You need practice, my son. (*He mimes cracking a whip.*) Practice. Practice.

The MONK *exits Stage Left practising cracking his whip.*

Lights now full up on ALMIRANTE'S *room. Regimental banners on the walls, a Spanish flag in one corner and clothes in a heap by the couch. The crucifix still hangs from the Flies.*

As MOTILLA *strides across to the couch,* TWO WOMEN *spring up with a shriek, throwing* ALMIRANTE *on the floor. They grab their clothes and rush out Stage Right.*

MOTILLA: Dumb gluttons! Public ledgers—open t' all parties! Why doest sin, my lord?

ALMIRANTE (*rising*): To please heaven, where there is more

rejoicing o'er one sinner who repenteth than o'er ninety-nine just men who need no repentance.

MOTILLA: You're a mutton-mongering fornicator.

ALMIRANTE: How canst I deny 't i' the face o' these Venus scars? I've taken so many mercury cures f' the pox, on a hot day I feel myself rising like a barometer. But I always confessed, repented, did hard penance f' 't like a good Christian.

MOTILLA: Now, as a good Christian, God wants you . . .

ALMIRANTE (*pulling on boot*): T' give up mutton-mongering. I need no holy vision t' know that.

MOTILLA: God wants you t' mutton-monger the Queen.

ALMIRANTE (*jumping up, boot half on*): *Mutton the Queen?*

MOTILLA: As Judah told Onan t' sleep wi' his brother's wife and raise up issue f' his brother so He commands you t' make the Queen pregnant afore she's examined. The King'll not do 't, believing 'tis done already.

ALMIRANTE (*pacing, his boot flapping*): How canst God speak o' muttoning? Using lust, lechery . . .?

MOTILLA: God oft time uses an ignoble tool f' a noble purpose.

ALMIRANTE: My honour, what o' my honour?

MOTILLA: Dishohour 't f' Spain and I'll keep Holy Day f' Judas. 'Tis my punishment. I sinned through pride. My soul cries out 'gainst this vileness but God's terrible voice thunders, '*Sin f' my sake*'.

ALMIRANTE: 'Tis impossible. The ghost o' a flea casn't hop from one heaving crotch t' another wi'out the Court hearing o' 't instantly.

MOTILLA: None'll hear o' 't. I'm the Queen's Confessor, and the King's. My lord, consider, if she's shown not t' be pregnant. The late Queen Louisa declared sterile was worm-meat two days after. Some believe 'twas a natural death, but I say she was cold poisoned. You speak much o' glory, my lord, now's the time t' unsheath your weapon and raise 't f' Queen Ana.

ALMIRANTE (*slowly*): If she's truly in such danger then my

weapon must be hers . . . (*They walk Down Stage and lights fade down.*) Royal bastards abound. Horns spread on Kings, Clowns and Turdmen alike. Women make all men equal. When am I t' be sent into the breech?

A large gauze is dropped Stage Centre. Projected onto it is the night sky.

MOTILLA: Tonight. Such things are best done at night. Darkness only frights children. 'Tis the pitiless day I find most terrible. E'en Lucifer, the morning star, turns pale afore the rising sun.

ALMIRANTE (*looking up*): There's Scorpio, there's Sagittarius and Centaurus. I once killed a man under that star . . . Tonight I change the history o' our world, decide the fate o' nations. 'Tis greatness o' a kind, a hole-i'-the-corner sort o' glory, eh?

MOTILLA (*looking up*): Canst see the stars shine and hear the planets wheel, making a divine murmur too soft f' outer ears? 'Tis the good Shepherd calming his flock from that lost cloud o' primordial dust beyond Neptune. List, list, he whispers, fainter than Uranus's moon. (*Whispering.*) 'I'm always here, loving, caring . . . come in my lambs, my lambikins . . . 'Oh, God's so gentle . . . do but listen . . . doest hear Him? . . . Hear him call us? . . . list . . . list . . . sshh . . . sshh . . .

They both listen intently. Then from far away the tiniest rustle of sound which grows into a long snigger.

As it swells to mirthless laughter, MOTILLA *and* ALMIRANTE *look frightened, shrink visibly and scuttle off Wings Left.*

SCENE X

DR BRAVO *and* GONGORA *enter Wings Right laughing, followed by his young assistant,* DR GELEEN, *with an instrument case.*

The night sky has faded and lights come up on the gauze Stage Centre, now a huge astrological chart with the Signs of the Zodiac. Nearby a table, with a bowl of water, a decanter, a chair and a brass armillary sphere.

DR BRAVO: He said: 'You doctors oft gi' wrong diagnoses. My mother was treated f' tertian fever and she died o' quatern ague.' 'Ne'er fear,' I replied. 'When I treat a patient f' tertian fever, he dies o' tertian fever.' And he did.

GONGORA: Wi'out a word o' thanks, I'm certain. They lack all gratitude and respect f' our arts. When I presented the notorious Marquesa de Gudannes wi' her astrological chart, I told her, 'I see new positions f' you, Madam'. 'Sitting or laying?' she leered back.

DR BRAVO: An open-legged wanton. She once gave me jus' seventy-two hours t' leave her bedchamber.

GONGORA: The stars 're retrograde. Jupiter's in adverse aspect t' Mercury. Madrid's become a compost o' quackery. In their misery the people turn t' magic; fortune-telling by numbers, fire, smoke, skulls, the guts o' dead birds. I see astrology, the great science of the Chaldeans and Greeks, falling into the hands o' midwives and gypsies peddling almanacs and Spanish fly.

DR GELEEN has laid out a sponge, a container of liquid and various heavy medical instruments on the table. DR BRAVO washes his hands in the bowl.

DR BRAVO: Confidence, Hermonymous. All authority's a matter o' confidence. We'll never lose 't if we do our duty wi'out fear or favour. (*He peers round, cannot find a towel so wipes his hands on his gown.*) Wi'out fear or favour.

GONGORA: 'Tis the only way, though the stars can be a stern mistress. (*He shows him a small manuscript.*) Your horoscope, Luis, wi' my projections f' the next twenty-four months. You'll note this most interesting conjunction o' planets at the time o' the square o' the progressed Uranus t' the Moon. Neptune by progression'll be i' opposition t' the Moon from the 10th House . . .

DR BRAVO: And what does that mean?

GONGORA: You'll be dead.

DR BRAVO: *Dead?*

As he grabs the manuscript DR GELEEN *suppresses a delighted grin.*

GONGORA: I fear yours was truly a horror-scope. But I must deal honestly. I casn't omit the Lord o' Death if he's in thy stars.

DR BRAVO: But is 't certain? I feel so well.

GONGORA: I've calculated the strength o' the lunaries, and malifics afflicting the Moon. But 'tis some twenty months hence and I'll be scanning the Heavens f' a sudden conjunction o' favouring signs.

DR BRAVO: That's possible?

GONGORA: If God wills it . . . Shall we proceed?

DR BRAVO: Procced? Oh, yes. (*He gestures,* GONGORA *sits.*) This 's more a task f' the Barber Surgeon.

GONGORA: That drunken sot! Saturn was rising in adverse aspect t' Venus at his nativity. He'd drink hemlock if 'twas in a bottle.

DR BRAVO: Which tooth's giving you pain?

GONGORA: None.

DR BRAVO: None? Then why do you want me t' pull 't out?

GONGORA: It gives no pain at present, but 'twill four weeks hence when Uranus'll be in Aries.

DR BRAVO: Ah, preventive medicine. If only my other patients 'd let me cure 'em afore they were ill, it'd be so much easier. (*He peers into* GONGORA'*s mouth.*) Which tooth'll be aching four weeks hence?

GONGORA (*pointing*): This one, according to astrological progression.

DR BRAVO *nods and crosses back to the table.*

GONGORA: You've heard the rumour concerning the Queen?

DR BRAVO (*gloomily*): Dead you say?

Behind his back DR GELEEN *nods gleefully.*

GONGORA: No, a miscarriage. She mayn't be pregnant. The

B—3

French Ambassador's already asked me t' cast up a new star-chart f' her. All Europe wonders.

DR BRAVO (*picking up the sponge with tongs*): 'Tis possible. A moist wind, a hard sneeze canst kill a mother's wandering womb. (*Soaks sponge in liquid.*) I warned 'em o' foul vapours from the uterus!

GONGORA: And I o' malicious aspects. Mars and Saturn canst suddenly appear t' darken the brightest futures.

DR BRAVO (*brightening*): Just as beneficial planets canst brighten a dark 'un, eh? If the stars've turned against the Queen they couldst as easily turn i' my favour. If she's barren, there's hope.

GONGORA: Your future's dark, the malifics . . . *ugh*.

DR BRAVO *slaps the opiate sponge in his face and holds it there.* GONGORA *waves his arms feebly then slumps back, mouth open.*

DR BRAVO *gives the tongs and sponge to* DR GELEEN, *picks up a heavy tool with a curved end called a 'pelican' and inserts it into* GONGORA's *mouth.*

DR BRAVO (*muttering*): Dead . . . Not the word o' a friend. Expect words o' cheer from a friend, *ahh*. (*He pulls, peers short-sightedly at the extracted tooth on the end of the tool, then into* GONGORA's *mouth.*) Hhhmmm, that's not right. (*He throws the tooth away and inserts the tool again.*) Dead . . . He wants me dead and t' be thanked f' it . . . *ahh* (*He pulls again, stares at the tooth and at the mouth.*) Hhmm . . . couple more f' luck. (*He tosses the tooth away and levers two more out.*) Dead . . . Dead . . . (*Holding up the last tooth in triumph.*) That's the work o' a true friend.

He crosses back to the table whilst DR GELEEN *packs up the equipment.* GONGORA *groans loudly.* DR BRAVO *pours a drink, gulps it down himself, and continues drinking.*

GONGORA: M' teeth, m' teeth. I've been robbed . . . (*He leaps up and staggers about, still dazed.*) Turn out the lights and let me see my stars! *Aaaaaa*, Saturn's i' the 12th House, the House o' Sorrow! Betrayals, treacheries, plots, deaths i' the dark, brightness falls away . . . (*The light fades.*) They're dead molars out there, the Saviour's served notice, this peregrine planet, those stars, that galaxy, this universe's being sucked into a great hole which sucks itself into itself at last, *whoosh*, goodnight, goodnight . . . (*The stars are gone: darkness and one frightened voice.*) *Aiee*, where 're my teeth my stars? *Aieee* I beat my empty gums and feel the caverns where my teeth were. *Aieee* 'tis the end o' creation!

SCENE XI

Lights up on QUEEN ANA's *Bedchamber. Drapes with flights of angels cover the walls. A four-poster bed Up Stage Centre, to the right of it a wardrobe. Stage Right the door to the corridor and below it a dressing table. A table Stage Centre, two trunks, one overflowing with gold plates and trinkets, Stage Left. Tall candleholders by the walls.*
ANA *in a voluminous dark nightgown is Down Stage Right with* MOTILLA, *who clasps a Bible: The* PARROT *is on a perch nearby.*

MOTILLA: Save us, Your Majesty, as Judith saved the Israelites, anointing herself in sweet oils, t' enter Haloferne's bed. Thou must do thy duty as a Queen, lay back . . .
    A knock on the door Stage Right. MOTILLA *stops talking instantly and pretends to read the Bible as the* FIRST LADY-IN-WAITING *enters, carrying a hot drink.*
    ANA *waves her away impatiently. She curtsies and withdraws.*
MOTILLA: . . . grit thy teeth, spread thy thighs wide as oysters at moon's zenith and think o' Spain.
ANA: But if we shouldst . . .?
    Another knock. ANA *stops talking as the* SECOND LADY-IN-WAITING *enters with a lace nightcap; again* ANA *waves her out.*
ANA: . . . fail. Doest know what you ask? T' be serviced in the service o' God is hard enough, but Father, the Almirante de Castilla isn't e'en o' royal blood.
PARROT: *Unclean, unclean. Leprosy and . . .*

Another knock: The PARROT *immediately stops talking as the* THIRD LADY-IN-WAITING *enters and curtsies. Whilst* MOTILLA *and* ANA *pretend to be praying she turns down the bedclothes and exits.*

PARROT: *. . . loose bowels. Crrah, crrah.*

MOTILLA: Though not o' royal blood, the Almirante is a true grandee and perfect Knight and his male bastards 're legion. (*Neither hears the knock or sees the* FOURTH LADY-IN-WAITING *enter.*) You'll not find a champion more worthy t' enter the lists than the Almirante de Castilla.

ALMIRANTE: Here, Father.

ANA: By St Julian!

She jumps back in fright at the sight of an acutely embarrassed ALMIRANTE *dressed as the fourth Lady-in-Waiting, in farthingale and wig.*

ALMIRANTE: Father, this isn't the dress o' a gentleman.

MOTILLA: 'Tis a good disguise. What's t' be done must be done quickly. (*He crosses and locks the door.*) Whilst I pray, you lay.

ALMIRANTE: You're staying wi' us?

MOTILLA: F' Her Majesty's honour.

ANA: She that thinks upon her honour, needs no other guard upon her.

MOTILLA: She that hath a man upon her, ne'er thinks upon her honour. 'Twill be safer. No one will interrupt whilst I'm here t' see you committed adultery in godly fashion, wi'out sin. On pain o' thy immortal souls, there casn't be one jot o' pleasure in 't.

ANA: If you stay, the bed curtains must be drawn.

MOTILLA: F' modesty's sake only, Your Majesty. But I'll be listening hard f' sinful love-cries, sobs, gasps, squeaks, heavy breathing. All 're an anathema. Especially heavy breathing.

ALMIRANTE: What o' grunts?

MOTILLA: Grunts? Grunts . . .? I'll permit grunts that betoken honest effort, *ugh*, but not grunts o' joy, *ugghh*. No lustful grunts o' joy, *ugghh*.

ALMIRANTE *is struggling to get out of the farthingale and petticoats.* MOTILLA *goes to help and they become entangled.*

ALMIRANTE: The hooks, unhook the hooks. Father, you didn't tell me 'twould be a glory wi'out dignity.

MOTILLA: Jus' be thy noble self.

ALMIRANTE: This is not one o' my noble days.

PARROT: *Crrah Crrah.*

ANA *puts a curtained cage over the* PARROT *and unbuttons her nightgown.*

ANA: I'd planned counting my gold tonight. Now I've t' devote myself t' State business. My lord Almirante, your singular service to the King must go unrewarded. But if he couldst know o' 't—God forbid—he'd prove as grateful as I am.

ALMIRANTE (*head appearing from petticoats*): The family motto's: 'Officii fructus sit ipsum officium'—Let the reward of duty be duty itself.

He finally steps out of his petticoats and stands in his underwear. On the opposite side of the bed ANA *waits tensely in her thick nightdress as he bows.*

ALMIRANTE: Your Majesty.

ANA *gets into bed, followed by* ALMIRANTE.

ANA: In the circumstances, you may call me Madam.

MOTILLA: Have a care, Your Majesty. There must be no undue familiarity 'twixt you that could give rise t' scandal. Only bodily contacts're permitted and that but o' vile necessity. Oh, that we could procreate like trees, wi'out conjunction! Ripple no muscles during coitus, Your Majesty. You must assume the missionary position as laid down by Thomas Aquinas: flat on thy back and motionless throughout. All other positions're sinful and barren f' the semen falls out when you move lustfully. 'Tis why God punishes us and Spain lies barren. No heat, no satisfaction, my lord. And only as much desire as needed t' raise thy standard bolt-high. Remember, 'tis an affair o' State.

MOTILLA *starts to close the bed-curtains.*

ANA: 'Twill be easy f' me. His Majesty's instrument's always been an instrument o' policy.

ALMIRANTE: 'Twill be hard f' me, wi' your care-causing beauty: mouth smelling o' mint and wild thyme; lips only meant t' gather kisses in.

ANA: Is that the language lovers speak? I've ne'er fallen 'cept i' the falling sickness. Then I was swept up into burning blue and gold. Oh the light, the light! Is that as love is?

ALMIRANTE: Yes. Love's an epilepsy too, its sufferers eat fire, see visions, dissolve time and flesh, moan, cry out, *aaahh aaahh.*

ANA: *Aaaahh? Aaahh?*

ALMIRANTE: *Aaaahh aaaaaaaahhhh.*

ANA: *Aaaahh aaaaaaaahhhh.*

He raises his hands and ANA *places her palms against his as* MOTILLA *shuts the last bed-curtain.*

MOTILLA kneels to pray. There is the tell-tale creaking of the bed. He listens intently.

MOTILLA (*low*): I can hear. You're both *breathing* . . . Fight 't, my children. Grunts . . . only grunts.

A series of short grunts from the bed. MOTILLA *nods, satisfied, and returns to his prayers.*

Suddenly there is a loud knocking on the door. MOTILLA *leaps up and* ANA's *and* ALMIRANTE's *flushed and frightened faces appear between the curtains. Whilst* MOTILLA *crosses to the door* ANA *clambers down, pushes* ALMIRANTE *back out of sight and throws on her dressing gown.*

She signals. MOTILLA *opens the door and* CARLOS *staggers in wearing a black nightcap and a gown over his nightshirt. He carries a lantern and bottle.*

CARLOS: Maaama . . . Maaama's been TALKING all night, clack-clack-clack, she hath the true gift o' tongues. I'll lie wi' m' wife t' show where my TRUE feelings lie.

They tense as he puts the lantern on the table and the bottle on the floor by the bed.

ANA: We're unprepared f' thy coming.

MOTILLA: And in the middle o' evening prayers, Your Majesty.

CARLOS: III'll pray too.

He crosses and kneels Stage Right in front of MOTILLA, *with his back to the bed.* ANA *joins him.* MOTILLA *directs his prayer over their heads to* ALMIRANTE *hidden in the bed.*

MOTILLA: We pray to the Lord Almighty whose merciless eye sees all. We canst not hide f' ever in one place, though we put on many *disguises.* (ALMIRANTE's *hand appears from between the bed-curtains to pick up his farthingale, but only manages to snatch up the wig.*) Repent and seize the opportunity t' escape his wrath. Lord God, their divine Majesties humbly kneel and close their eyes afore the splendour o' thy radiant presence. (CARLOS *and* ANA *shut their eyes.*) Unseeing i' the darkness they trust blindly in Thee. The sinner must come forth now and . . .

Even as the bed-curtains start to part, there is a knock on the door and ANA *and* CARLOS *open their eyes to see a slightly drunk* RAFAEL *hurrying in, bowing.*

RAFAEL: Sire, the Queen Mother comes at a gallop.

CARLOS (*jumping up*): Hide me!

Before the others can stop him he rushes to the bed and dives in, closing the curtains behind him. ANA *and* MOTILLA *brace themselves. But nothing happens.*

RAFAEL: I'd best hide too, else she'll know the King's here.

As he quickly clambers into one of the trunks Stage Left and ANA *and* MOTILLA *stare bewildered at the silent bed, there is a perfunctory knock and* MARIANA *enters.* ANA *immediately whips off the* PARROT's *curtained cage; the bird squawks raucously at the sight of* MARIANA *sweeping down to them.*

PARROT: 'Tis Medusa's Mother. Crrah Crrah.

MARIANA: I'll strangle that pestilential fowl. You've trained him t' bait me.

ANA: No, he doeth 't from instinct. You've no right here, Madam.

MOTILLA: We're trying t' pray.

MARIANA: I find no difficulty. Pray continue praying, Father.

   MOTILLA *and* ANA *exchange glances.*

MOTILLA: Bow down thy heads. (*The women look down.*) F' He hath hidden Himself away from our sight. We knoweth not where He's at. We've lost Him. Only show Thyself . . . show Thyself . . . *show Thyself dammit.* (ALMIRANTE'*s head appears from under the foot of the bed.*) We give thanks, Lord. (ANA *looks up, sees* ALMIRANTE *and hastily points to the wardrobe before looking down again.*) 'Benedicto Dei omnipoténtes Patris et Fílii . . .' (*As* ALMIRANTE *wriggles out,* CARLOS *peers from behind the bed curtains and* RAFAEL *from the trunk; they do not see him, only* MOTILLA *signalling frantically for them to get back; they do so but* ALMIRANTE *thinks the signal's for him and slides back also.*) 'et Spiritus Sancti descendat super te et máneat semper. Amen.'

ANA: You've come t' curse my womb, blast my child.

MARIANA: I saw my son come into thy bedchamber. Where's he hiding?

ANA: Where else would His Majesty, Carlos II o' Spain and the Dependencies, Grand Master o' the Golden Fleece, Defender o' the Faith, hide, but under his wife's bed. Look!

   Before MOTILLA *can warn her that* ALMIRANTE *is still there,* ANA *crosses excitedly and starts to lift the counterpane hanging over the foot of the bed.* MARIANA *moves to her.*

MARIANA: As a child Carlos was most prone t' hide . . . in wardrobes.

   She darts Up Stage and flings open the wardrobe. ANA *gives an involuntary cry of fright.* ALMIRANTE, CARLOS *and* RAFAEL *look out from their hiding places for a second, then disappear as* MARIANA *looks round. To cover her confusion* ANA *clutches her stomach and groans.*

   MOTILLA *guides her to the dressing table Stage Right; she sits.*

MOTILLA: Ma'am, Her Majesty's condition 's most delicate—please go.

PARROT: *Good-night ladies, 'tis time t' say 'night 'night.*

MARIANA (*crossing*): She's weak-blooded. 'Tis her clapped out
German strain. When I was heavy wi' Carlos I stood f' six
hours gi'ing audience t' the Duke o' Palamo.

As they stand Stage Right, ALMIRANTE *seizes his chance and
propels himself out from under the bed and into the wardrobe.
Immediately after* CARLOS *slips down into* ALMIRANTE's *former
hiding place and* RAFAEL *dives into* CARLOS's *place in the bed.
There is a knock and* BELEPSCH *enters quickly with a long candle-
snuffer. She is shocked at seeing the Queen.*

BELEPSCH: Your Majesty, 'tis gone eight! Etiquette demands
you be in bed long since.

ANA: Blame Her Royal Highness, here. You'll suffer f' this,
Madam.

MARIANA: You're wasting your breath—and that's no great
loss. 'Tis between me and my son. When I'm gone he'll creep
out and you'll mould his melting mind 'gainst me.

BELEPSCH sees ALMIRANTE's *farthingale on the floor, clucks
disapprovingly, picks it up and opens the wardrobe to put it away.
As she is holding the bulky dress in front of her, she does not see
the rigid figure of* ALMIRANTE *flattening himself against the back
of the wardrobe, but* ANA *does.*

ANA: Countess Belepsch! (BELEPSCH *turns quickly.*) The candles.
Snuff out the candles.

Without looking, BELEPSCH *quickly dumps the farthingale on
top of* ALMIRANTE, *closes the door and begins snuffing out the
candle. The* PARROT *gives a piercing shriek and snores loudly.*
ANA *rises and puts the curtained cage over the bird.*

ANA: Madam Thornback, if thou doesn't leave I'll've the
pleasure o' seeing the Attendants throw you out.

MARIANA: Carlos, you're here, Carlos! I canst smell you, I'm
your Mother.

She darts across to the bed and tears open the curtains. It is empty.

MOTILLA: Come, Ma'am. The Queen retires. So must you—
permanently—after this night's work.

As he guides her firmly to the exit, CARLOS *and* RAFAEL *peer*
B—3*

momentarily out from under the bed. MARIANA *and* MOTILLA *pause in the doorway and look back at* ANA, *who has taken off her dressing gown and is in bed.*

MOTILLA: God grant thee pleasant slumber, Your Majesty.

MARIANA: Carlos. Son. Don't listen t' her, Carlos . . . Carlos . . . Carlos . . .

They exit. BELEPSCH *snuffs out the last candle, curtsies in the doorway and follows them out.*

The room is in darkness except for the tiniest spot of light from the lantern on the table.

Silence, then the sound of scampering in the darkness, doors opening and closing, nervous whisperings: 'Who's that?' . . . ''tis me.' . . . 'Who's me?' . . . *A frightened gasp, more scurryings, a muffled curse, then* ANA *appears by the table and turns up the lantern light. She peers round, hears something and flits away.*

First a woebegone ALMIRANTE *in battered farthingale and lop-sided wig and then an absurd night-shirted* CARLOS *stagger in quick succession in and out of the pool of light. Next* RAFAEL *in a woman's hat tip-toes past stealthily. Noticing the audience he stops, stares at them then goes into a frenetic 'Charleston' dance, legs kicking, arms waving wildly. Just as suddenly he 'freezes' in mid-motion, then darts away into the darkness.*

MOTILLA *appears next and turns the lantern full up to light the room and show an extraordinary glimpse of banging doors and disappearing figures:* RAFAEL *into the trunk,* ALMIRANTE *into the wardrobe.* ANA *in the bed and* CARLOS *under it. About to speak,* MOTILLA *hears something and turns the lantern right down.*

Darkness . . . Breathing . . . Suddenly two lantern lights full up to show MOTILLA *and* MARIANA *standing face to face Down Stage Centre, lanterns in their hands.*

MARIANA (*low*): *Lucifer.*

MOTILLA (*low*): *Old Serpent.* I was waiting f' thee, Ma'am. (*Guides her out.*) I shall inform the King and the Council you came back to fright the Queen out o' her wits and child.

MARIANA (*low*): No, 'twas t' see my Carlos. (*A bump from the wardrobe.*) You heard 't?

MOTILLA (*low*): Nothing. Brain fever.

Another bump from the wardrobe.

MARIANA (*low*): Brain fever? 'Tis my Carlos!

She goes towards the wardrobe. MOTILLA *pulls her back and they struggle, trying not to make a sound.*

MOTILLA (*low*): By the stigmas and the sorrows, I swear 't isn't His Majesty.

MARIANA (*low*): Then 'tis somebody else. Plots. Treacheries. Assignations. Now 'tis my turn t' turn and turn again! *Crrah crrah.*

Breaking away, she rushes to the wardrobe and flings it open. She screams and steps aside in fright, to reveal ANA, *smiling. foolishly, swaying and falling out in a faint.* CARLOS *and* RAFAEL *rush from their hiding places in the bed and trunk.*

CARLOS: Whaaaa . . .?

MARIANA: Carlos, I want t' know; what were you doing in your wife's bed?!

RAFAEL: I'll fetch Attendants.

MOTILLA: T' what purpose? They casn't touch the Queen, e'en if she be dying.

CARLOS: Whaaaa . . .? Whaaaa . . .?

MARIANA: Why didst you hide from me, Carlos? Sometimes I think I've failed you as a Mother.

ANA *suddenly groans, staggers up and collapses at the foot of the bed.*

ANA (*clutching stomach*): Dead. It's dead. My child's dead. Our child's dead, Carlos! That witch hath frighted him away, Carlos. I've lost him, Carlos! He's returned t' God—t' God— t' God . . . He's gone. I'm emptied.

As MOTILLA *hurries out,* CARLOS *spins slowly round and round, his mouth wide open.*

MARIANA: 'Tis a trick 'gainst me, Carlos, assassins behind every bush wi' honey in their mouths, razors in their hands, Jesu, Jesu save me from their little pinking eyes!

RAFAEL: Come Sire, the Queen's surely mistaken.

ANA (*rocking gently and singing*): 'Schlaf, Kinderl, schlaf!/Dein Vater ist ein Graf,/Dein Mutter ist ein Bauerndirn,/Soll ihr Kinderl selber wiegn./Schlaf, Kinderl, schlaf!'

CARLOS: *Maaamaaaahhh . . .*

He leaps up on the bedcurtains and hangs with one hand from them, gibbering 'Maamaa . . . Maamaa'.

As RAFAEL *and* MARIANA *rush to him,* ALMIRANTE *creeps out from under the dressing table and using the seat as a cover, makes for the exit.* RAFAEL *turns and sees him as he abandons the seat and dives out.*

RAFAEL stares and is about to follow him when CARLOS *suddenly leaps down onto* MARIANA *and starts to throttle her.*

RAFAEL: Sire, you'll do thyself an injury.

As MARIANA *gasps and croaks,* DR BRAVO *rushes in with* MOTILLA.

DR BRAVO: Ne'er fear, Sire, Bravo's here, *ahhh.*

He goes flying over the dressing-table seat left in his path. Smirking, DR GELEEN *helps him up whilst* MARIANA *and* CARLOS *struggle violently.*

MOTILLA: Sire, leave her t' the terrible mercy o' God.

CARLOS lets go of MARIANA *who staggers away, feeling her neck, and joins* DR BRAVO *beside* ANA.

CARLOS: Doeth mmmm child live? Doeth he? Is he? Whaaa good's a King wi'out an heir whaa . . .

DR BRAVO: 'Tis in God's hands. He maketh the stars change, babes die, old men live on. We'll soon know the best and the worst.

He guides ANA *onto the bed and* DR GELEEN *closes the bedcurtains round them.*

Lights dim down to Spot on CARLOS. *A choir sings softly the Holy Innocents Day Hymn: 'Salvete flores martyrum.'*

CARLOS: Lord 've mercy, save my son. IIIII'll beeee penitent,

thorned, pierced, scourged, hammered, spat on oooooonly
hoist me high t' Theeeeeee . . .

CARLOS *lets out a great cry of despair. The bright Spot flickers
and he shakes convulsively as he falls into an epileptic fit. His
grotesque twistings and jerkings quickly reach a pitch of intensity,
then suddenly die away and the flicker stops.*

Darkness except for the Spot on CARLOS *lying curled up Down
Stage Centre in a foetus position.*

He rises, coldly furious, in a state of post-epileptic automation.

CARLOS: Dead? Is my child dead?

I'll wound the earth, kill the sun, stamp out
the stars,
Storm the vault o' heaven and drag that tit-face
tyrant, God,
Down by his greasy locks, f' taking back my child.
(Not his t' take, only t' give, not t' take.)
I'll loose war and death in Paradise.
There'll be wronged men enough t' march wi' me,
Under a black flag, skull and broken bones rampant.
And the motto: 'Resistance t' tyrants is obedience
t' God.'

Doest hear me, dung-heap!
My maw-walloping, cow-hearted, copper-arsed,
crab-lousy,
Jolter-headed, herring-gutted, cock-pimping, bum-
fiddling, divine shit-shack!
Answer me, answer me!
There's no difference 'tween prayers and curses,
He's long since fled.
Heaven's as empty as her belly;
There is no God.

Thunder, a streak of lightning and a great voice booms:

GOD' VOICE: YES THERE IS.

CARLOS: I've prayed t' you. Where's my son?

Another streak of lightning.

GOD'S VOICE (*wearily*): NO SON—ONLY LIGHTNING.
Thunder, another streak of lightning and CARLOS *collapses. The attack is over.*

SCENE XII

MOTILLA *appears in the Spot behind* CARLOS.

CARLOS: WWWWWhy do I suffer?
MOTILLA: 'Cause thou art a man. You casn't sin wi'out being evil, evil wi'out being degraded, degraded wi'out being punished, punished wi'out being *guilty*. We're conceived in iniquity. Man alone knows 't, 'tis his glory and his shame. The wise cry out 'Who shall deliver me?' The weak surrender and call their cowardice happiness.
CARLOS: WWWWWhy do I suffer?
MOTILLA: As punishment. All earthly and spiritual order rest on punishment. As Your Majesty punishes criminals, so His Divine Majesty punishes sinners. Only his whips and racks're diseases and death. Diseases're sins made manifest, passed down generation t' generation. Sire, we stink and putrify from the sins o' our fathers.
CARLOS: WWWWWhy do I suffer?
MOTILLA: Out o' love. The greater the sin, the greater God's concern, the greater pain needed t' cut 't out. Knives, forceps, saws 're terrible instruments o' torture. But in the hands o' the skilled physicians they save our bodies. So God saves our souls wi' His instruments; His tumours, goitres, cancers. Can a broken limb be restored wi'out agony? A haemorrhage wi'out privation, a cancerous growth wi'out the bloody knife? Can a damned soul be brought t' salvation wi'out the healing pain?
CARLOS: Mercy, mercy, mercy!
MOTILLA: God shows His mercy only by punishing us i' this world where pain hath an end, rather than the next, where 'tis

everlasting. Serve and fear Him. 'Tis useless t' rebel or flee. He is omnipotent and the Empire o' grief is everywhere.

A CANTOR *chants the responsory from the Funeral Service:* 'Subvenite Sancti Dei occurite, Angeli Domine . . .' *as* CARLOS *and* MOTILLA *disappear Up Stage.*

SCENE XIII

Lights up on the Throne-Room.
Still in his nightdress, CARLOS *is slumped on the Throne Up Stage Centre.* ANA *and* MARIANA *stand either side of him, whilst* RAFAEL *sits at his feet. The members of the Council of State,* PONTOCARRERO, ALMIRANTE, MONTERREY, ALBA *and* TORRES, *are formally positioned below the steps of the rostrum.*

PONTOCARRERO: We've become a nation o' enchanted men, outside the natural order: rich but poor, ruined but intact, all our beginnings an end. Much happens and nothing changes; we move forward and stand still; act and do nothing. The Queen's miscarriage compels you t' make a decision, Sire. The succession. The French army in Catalonia's t' move 'gainst us'less you name Philip Bourbon heir, the House o' Austria still presses f' Archduke Charles whilst Bavaria waits on José.

ALMIRANTE: But first the guilty must be punished, Sire. The Royal Physician's confirmed our Queen was frighted out o' her pregnancy. I ask, who hated her, who pursued her e'en t' her bedchamber? (*All look at* MARIANA.) My lords, I move the Queen Mother be found guilty o' the Queen's miscarriage and humbly recommend His Majesty exile her from Madrid. Though I be broken f' 't, I must speak out. My body's but a tool t' be used i' the service o' my King.

RAFAEL: What tool doest use t' service the Queen?

ALMIRANTE: My heart. My lords . . .?

The OTHERS *look up at* CARLOS *for a lead, but he remains slumped on the throne.* MARIANA *stares implacably down at them. They hesitate.*

ANA: Commit. If thou doesn't commit you jus' take up space. Commit. Rid me o' her. COMMIT.

ALBA, TORRES *and* MONTERREY *raise their hands. All look at* PONTOCARRERO.

PONTOCARRERO: Lower your hands, my lords. We're all agreed the Queen Mother's guilty . . . As I am . . . As we all are. The blame's not i' one breast. This nation, chosen by God t' be the defender o' the true Faith, hath proved unworthy. So we're punished. But Our Saviour'll forgive his children and end their humiliation and impotence if they do but show Him a sign o' their love and repentance.

CARLOS: Hooooow?

PONTOCARRERO: By asking the Suprema t' sanction a Day o' Contrition, an Act o' Faith, a Festival o' Light, an Auto de fe!

CARLOS: Auto dddddd fe?

PONTOCARRERO *nods confidently.* ANA *and* ALMIRANTE *exchange uneasy glances.*

PONTOCARRERO: At a stroke 'twill rouse our armies, dismay our enemies, curb all dissent, unite the nation . . .

MARIANA: And, God willing, strengthen thy loins. Your father was always stimulated by the fires o' an auto de fe. Thy late brother, Prince Prospero, was conceived on the night o' one such spectacular.

ANA: What o' my miscarriage, her banishment?!

CARLOS: Auto ddddd?

ALMIRANTE: Sire, afore we can organize any auto de fe, we must organize the relief of Barcelona from an attack o' the French.

RAFAEL: You couldn't organize the relief o' your bowels from an attack o' the piles.

ANA: What o' HER!

CARLOS (*staggering up*): Shouldst weeee . . .? shouldst weeeee ask the Suprema . . .? Whaaa does my Council sss t' an auto de fe . . . whaaa . . .? Advise . . .

MONTERREY: I'm 'gainst 't, Sire. An auto de fe's an expensive undertaking. (*The drapes Stage Right part and a six-spoke Torture-wheel, with a* PRISONER *strapped to it, is placed Down Stage Left by two hooded Dominican* MONKS.) True, the common people'd give freely, preferring burnings t' bread, but the bulk o' the money'd come from us grandees. No, Sire, the time's not ripe.

He is gently escorted off by the two MONKS. *There is the sound of a large animal panting.*

TORRES: Remember the first aphorism o' Hippocrates, Sire: 'Ars Longa, Vita Brevis'. The Dutch grow tulips; the French dance the minuet; Spaniards burn heretics. The auto de fe is more than jus' a national pastime, 'tis a true folk art. (*Drapes Stage Right part again and the* DOMINICANS *wheel in an Iron Maiden—a hollow wooden case, the inside lid studden with spikes.*) All o'er Europe dissenters're being flayed and crucified. But crudely, wi'out the dramatic genius Spaniards bring t' killing f' their God. No, Sire, 't mustn't be rushed into.

The two MONKS *exit with* TORRES *between them. The panting grows louder, the lights brighter.*

ALBA: 'Twould besmirch our honour if the auto weren't staged wi' true pomp. (*Drapes Stage Left part and a horizontal rack with a* PRISONER *spreadeagled on it is wheeled Down Stage Left by two more hooded Dominican* MONKS.) Madrid's not seen a public auto f' a decade. Like as all that's best, 'tas dropped from fashion. O' course Castille and Serena keep the tradition alive. But however worthy, they're essentially provincial shows: quantity not quality. A Royal auto de fe's different and needs months t' prepare. No, Sire, we must think long on the matter.

He is escorted out between the two MONKS.

ANA: All say the same. The answer's no, Carlos. No auto de fe. The answer's no, no, no, no . . .

Though CARLOS *nods vigorously in agreement with* ANA *and* ALMIRANTE, PONTOCARRERO *smiles confidently at* MARIANA.

*As they continue nodding and the sound of panting grows louder
and louder, the throne rostrum revolves carrying* CARLOS, ANA,
MARIANA, ALMIRANTE *and* RAFAEL *out of sight whilst the
drapes are taken up to reveal dungeon walls.*

MONKS *place spare furnishings as the panting increases, then
suddenly stops.*

SCENE XIV

PONTOCARRERO *calmly sniffs a scented handkerchief and looks
around the Torture Chamber of the Spanish Inquisition, with its
Wheel, Rack and Iron Maiden.*
*The entrance door is Up Stage Centre at the top of a flight of stairs
(part of the back of the rostrum) that curves Down Stage Right. At
the bottom a* PRISONER *hangs in chains from an armetarium on the
wall. Red hot pokers and rods are being heated in a brazier Stage
Centre next to a stained stone slab serving as a table. Stage Left a
low archway leads to another part of the dungeon.*
ALCALA *enters briskly through it, with his son* GOMEZ. *Middle-aged
and dignified, he wears a leather skull-cap and smock with a red
cross on the front, and carries a brace of rats. His son is similarly
dressed but carries a bucket and brush.*

ALCALA: Your Eminence.
   Crossing quickly they kneel and kiss PONTOCARRERO's *hand.
   He gestures and they rise.* ALCALA *gives* GOMEZ *the rats to throw
   into the brazier.*
PONTOCARRERO: How comes the auto de fe?
ALCALA: As Chief Torturer t' the Holy Office I've found 'tis
   always fatal t' hurry such matters.
GOMEZ: Father! Look, blood!
   He is pointing to a stain on the floor by the Wheel. ALCALA
   crosses quickly and examines it.
ALCALA (*to* PRISONER *on the Wheel*): You've been *bleeding*

again! We spend the night cleaning up your mess and you
start t' bleed all over the place. (*The* PRISONER *groans*.) That's
no excuse.

    MOTILLA *enters Stage Left.*

MOTILLA: Your Eminence.

PONTOCARRERO: Father.

MOTILLA: I was inspecting the cells on behalf o' the Inquisitor-
General.

PONTOCARRERO: And I on behalf o' His Majesty.

    They walk round slowly, inspecting the chamber as ALCALA *and*
GOMEZ *carry a roll of carpet up the steps.*

MOTILLA: 'Twas a neat device, Your Eminence, for diverting
attention from the Queen Mother. Even I had t' support the
holding o' an auto de fe.

PONTOCARRERO: Naturally. Nine months after the last auto
generale, there was an almighty outcrop o' births.

MOTILLA: The stench o' burning flesh seems but t' stir up our
vile lust f' life.

    ALCALA *and* GOMEZ *unroll the red carpet down the steps.*

PONTOCARRERO: Pray 'twill stir up His Majesty. I trust you're
mindful o' the great service I've done your Order i' suggesting
this auto.

MOTILLA: Beware o' Jesuits bearing gifts.

PONTOCARRERO: Ne'er fear, the auto'll be a blazing triumph.
Your Inquisitor-General's proved himself many times o'er.
His Holiness loves him, as Cardinal Borgia once loved Fray
Torquemanda, f' the remorselessness o' his punishments,
the strength o' his severity and the courage o' his pitilessness.

    *The door Up Stage Centre is thrown open by two hooded
Dominican* MONKS *dressed in the black robe of the Inquisition.*
ALCALA *and* GOMEZ, *fixing the carpet at the foot of the stairs,
bow their heads.*

ALCALA: The Inquisitor-General. (*To* PRISONERS.) Show
respect there.

    A tapping sound and the Inquisitor-General, VALLADARES, *is framed in the doorway. The wizened old man, bent with arthritis, hobbles beady-eyed down the stairs on two sticks.*

VALLADARES: 'Tis good t' see thee here at last, Your Eminence. I've been trying f' years t' arrange f' you to visit the cells o' the Inquisition.

PONTOCARRERO: I've been aware o' 't, my dear Valladares. But now I must report t' the King. God be with thee, Fathers.

They bow their heads as he goes quickly up the stairs and exits.

VALLADARES: Damnable Jesuits! Would we had another Fray Alonso t' pursue 'em all t' the fires.

MOTILLA: His Eminence 's a careful man. He neglects his duties as a priest but bears no taint o' heresy.

VALLADARES: All men 're tainted, 'tis the worm i' the bud. I see 't everywhere; faces, voices, eyes, hands, the wind. We drowned in heresy: young, old, rich, poor, Cardinals, Captains, Viceroys, Governors, Princes, Kings—and in the darkest watches o' the night I e'en have doubts about His Holiness, Pope Innocent XII, himself!

MOTILLA: Morality should have 'ts fires too. His Eminence's allowed t' flourish under the purity o' his dogma.

VALLADARES: Look round and weep at Spain's decadence. This prison used t' bulge wi' the excommunicated limbs o' Satan, waiting t' be relaxed at the stake. Enough men and women t' fuel a dozen autos de fe. Now I've t' send t' Toledo. (ALCALA *offers him a parchment.*) What's this?

ALCALA: My list o' condemned penitents f' the auto de fe.

VALLADARES (*reading*): Eight blasphemers f' the galleys. Ten Judaizers t' be relaxed i' prison. Juan Martinez exhumed f' a heresy committed in 1495 . . . that's a rarity, the first ever two-hundred-year-old heretic t' be burned in Madrid. (*Hands list to* MOTILLA.) Should prove the basis o' a varied programme, wi' the burning alive o' our pertinacious Jew, Diego Lopez Duro, a fitting climax t' the festivities.

ALCALA: Duro's not for burning, Inquisitor-General.

VALLADARES: Take care, I consider a sense o' humour's a sure sign o' internal heresy.

ALCALA: 'Tis my honour t' report that last night, after five years' struggle wi' rack and hot irons, that pertinacious Jew, Lopez Duro, finally adjured, confessed and sang the praises o' the true Lord, Jesus Christ.

VALLADARES: What! Devil take him . . . Go bring me yer tardy convert.

ALCALA *bows and exits Stage Left.*

MOTILLA: If Duro's truly converted, he's earned God's mercy and must be garrotted at the stake afore the fires are lit, like the rest o' 'em. All penitents reconciled t' Christ must be strangled afore burning. Wi'out Duro we've no-one t' burn *alive.*

VALLADARES: And no time t' find a replacement. I was relying on Duro t' stand firm in his accursed heresy. Now he recants and dies too fast. Heretics used t' meet death with a fierce joyfulness. True, 't sprung from a devilish exultation o' sin and not the gentle humility o' the true martyr f' Christ. But they made a most satisfying spectacle. I still recall Raphael Valles i' the auto o' '85. Standing still as a bright statue, hair sheeted in flame, till he burst open and his hot tripes and trullibubs spilt out and all the time crying: 'Jehovah, Lord God o' Zion, the law o' Moses is the only true law, Jehovah, Jehovah . . .'

DURO: Jesu, Jesu, Jesu. Glory be t' the Father and t' the Son and t' the Holy Ghost.

ALCALA *enters proudly Stage Left with the exulting* LOPEZ DURO, *a bony man with matted beard, disintegrating loin cloth and chains.*

ALCALA: Inquisitor-General, this's Lopez Duro, once a vile Judaizer, now praise be t' God, a true believer.

VALLADARES: I'll be the judge o' his beliefs, (*he jabs the air with his stick*) AND YOURS AND YOURS AND YOURS. Go, join thy son. Gi' us warning o' the King's coming.

ALCALA *bows and joins* GOMEZ *who has been looking out the doorway at the top of the stairs.*

DURO: I-do-confess-I-was-a-Judaizer-who-didst-abominate-pork-and-winkles-and-didst-change-my-linen-drawers-and-light-candles-on-the-Sabbath-Now-I-believe-in-God-the-Father-Almighty-and-in-Jesus-Christ-His-Only-Son-our-Lord . . .

VALLADARES: Recant your new found faith!

DURO: *Recant?* But you've spent five years converting me t' Christ. Five years on the wheel, *confess, confess, adjure, adjure.* Tongue grated, hands splintered, toes hanging by a little skin, spirit broken wi' my bones. Oh Jesu spare me, spare me, I'll not recant.

VALLADARES: Do't then, f' Jesus. 'Twill do Him most good if you burn at the stake a *live* Jew rather than a *dead* Christian.

MOTILLA (*turning away*): Compromise, that old devil compromise.

VALLADARES: Relapse, and burn f' Christ! 'Twill be t' thy advantage.

DURO: 'Tis a trick t' test my faith. Testing, one-two-three-I-believe-in-God-the-Father-Almighty-and-in-Jesus-Christ-His-Only-Son-born . . . Advantage? What advantage?

VALLADARES: We hold your son on a burning offence. But the Inquisition, in 'ts mercy, could recognize his father's singular service t' the Faith and reduce the sentence t' perpetual exile.

DURO: 'Tis torture by hope. I don't believe thee . . . I don't believe . . . I don't believe . . .

VALLADARES: My last offer. Relapse and burn alive and your son'll be exiled wi' one hundred ducats.

DURO: Two hundred!

VALLADARES: Ingrate! Usurious pork-hating Jew! Not a ducat more I'll . . .

DURO: I-believe-in-God-the-Father-Almighty-i'-Jesus-Christ-His-Only-Son-Our-Lord-born . . .

VALLADARES: Two hundred.

DURO: How doest I know you'll deliver my son and money safe, afore I roast?

VALLADARES: How doest I know you'll not turn Christian again afore you burn? We must trust each other.

DURO: 'Tis a question of' faith.

GOMEZ: His Majesty! His Majesty approaches!

He and ALCALA *come down excitedly to wait at the foot of the stairs as an* ATTENDANT *appears in the doorway.*

ATTENDANT: His Most Catholic Majesty, Defender o' the Faith, Carlos o' Spain.

They kneel. CARLOS *enters quickly and goes careering down the steps followed by* PONTOCARRERO *and* FROYLAN.

CARLOS *gestures and the* OTHERS *rise. Smiling inanely he begins a quick tour of the chamber accompanied by* ALCALA *and* GOMEZ. *They cross to the* PRISONER *hanging from the wall Stage Right.*

CARLOS: GGG' t' see thee . . . er . . . er . . . (ALCALA *whispers in his ear.*) Master Domingo de la Cruz . . . lot o' weather we've been having . . . the heat . . . tttthink thyself MOST lu-lu-lucky this is the only cool place i' Madrid. (*The* PRISONER *nods feebly and* CARLOS *passes to the* PRISONER *on the Wheel.*) . . . er . . . uhm . . . (ALCALA *whispers again.*) Ahh . . . weeeee hear you maa good progress o'er thy heresy concerning . . . er . . . kkkkkeep 't UP . . .

2ND PRISONER (*croaking*): God bless thee, Sire.

CARLOS *crosses to the* PRISONER *on the rack Stage Left.*

CARLOS: Er . . . won't beeee long now . . .

3RD PRISONER: *Ahhhhhh.*

He screams in pain as CARLOS *accidentally knocks against the rack handle.* ALCALA *scowls at the* PRISONER.

CARLOS: Whaaa . . .? aaa . . . meee?

3RD PRISONER (*gasping*): 'Twas a great honour, Your Majesty.

CARLOS *moves Down Stage where* VALLADARES *and* MOTILLA *and* PONTOCARRERO *and* FROYLAN *stare coldly at each other whilst* DURO *looks on bemused.*

CARLOS: Aaa—Inspector-General . . . aaaall goes well? MUST . . . my last chance . . .

VALLADARES: We've grave problems, Sire.

FROYLAN: Can my staff help the Holy Office o'er transportation, catering, extra supplies o' wood?

PONTOCARRERO: I'm certain the Inquisitor-General'd resent any interference from the Society o' Jesus. He'll do his best, as always. He knows there's more at stake than jus 'a few heretics. Spain's asking God t' renew His covenant wi' His people by making Their Majesties fertile again.

ALCALA: Sire, the signs're good. After five years, this most obstinate Jew, Lopez Duro's at last become reconciled t' Jesus Christ.

CARLOS: Maaaster Torturer, waaa words wi' thee . . .

> *They all bow.* PONTOCARRERO *and* FROYLAN *retire up, Stage Right to watch suspiciously* VALLADARES *and* MOTILLA, *Up Stage Left, whispering urgently to* DURO. GOMEZ *hovers near his proud father.*

ALCALA: Your Majesty?

CARLOS: Tell mmmmm about death.

ALCALA: *Death?* Sire, you wrong me! I know nothing o' death, 'cept what all men know. I'm Spain's Chief Torturer, not Executioner. I bring penitents t' the threshold o' death, but ne'er o'er, else their souls 'd escape t' Hell and be lost f' Christ. Men die here, but only through accident, weakness, sheer perversity on their part. I've no extra knowledge o' death. Pain's my province. I can tell thee o' pain, Sire, and its outrider, fear.

CARLOS: I know pain, paaaa's my familiar tooo. Sleeping— waking paaaa, eating—drinking paaaa, all-the-time paaaa; e'en when 't doesn't hurt I feel paaaa. Whaaa canst you tell me o' paaain?

ALCALA: 'Tis my craft, Sire. 'Stead o' hard metal I work soft flesh into precious ornaments f' Our Lord. The goldsmiths o' Silos took three years t' prepare a golden Chalice f' St Dominic

I took five t' prepare the body of the Jew, Lopez Duro, f'
Jesus Christ. Gi'en time, all men canst be broken and re-made.
But 'tis no task for fresh-faced understrappers. My son
Gomez's a promising lad, but as yet lacks all patience. There's
so much t' learn, Sire. What point o' pain t' attack—eyelid,
tongue, spine, armpit. What degree o' pain t' apply. Short
bursts produce the best results, f' they're followed by long
periods o' ease. 'Tis in this pain-free time the penitent suffers
most, consumed wi' fear o' pain's return, pain past, pain t'
come, flesh's pain, mind's pain. 'Tis the mind that sets the
flesh aquiver, knowing what has been and will be endured.
Then a feather-touch can set 'em screaming. Sire, I long t' tell
the world o' the godly work we do here, the guilty finding
repentance, the innocent, a true strengthening o' faith. This
cell's an altar t' the suffering Christ! Here we feel the thorn's
prick, taste His sacred wounds streaming—*they stream, they
stream*: chastiser and chastised merging i' the blessed com-
munion o' pain! The joyful vocation o' suffering! (*He seizes
a hot iron rod and slaps it on his bare arm: his flesh sizzles.*) But
that joy's as nothing t' the joy o' bringing such souls as Lopez
Duro t' salvation. How I cried in triumph when his blood
mingled wi' my sweat and he cried, 'I believe in the Father,
Son and Holy Ghost, Virgin Mary, Mother o' God' and I
cried 'Hallelujah, I believe, I believe . . .'

DURO: . . . that the law o' Moses is the only true law, Oh Lord
God o' Zion! (*Hebraically chanting the Kaddish Prayer.*) 'B'olmo
Rabbo Shmey V'yiskadash Yisgadal/Malchusej V'yamlich
Chir'usey Dee-vro/Beis D'chol Uu'chayez Uu'yomeichon
B'chayeichon . . .'

He staggers forward waving his arms. All stare at him:
VALLADARES, MOTILLA *in relief, the* OTHERS *in varying
degrees of horror.*

ALCALA: NO! Not a relapse, here i' front o' the King! You
casn't slide back into heresy. 'Tis sheer bloody-mindedness.
Think o' me.

VALLADARES: As I suspected, his heresy's too deep rooted t' be rooted out in a mere five years. Prepare him f' Jesus and St Paul!

GOMEZ *bundles* DURO *out Stage Left, still chanting ecstatically.*

CARLOS: Whaaa o' the AUTO . . .?!

VALLADARES: Ne'er fear, Sire, such difficulties act as a spur, t' the godly. I'll cauterize Spain's wounds. Mere words die i' the air, but the vision o' burnt and blistering flesh commands a lasting obedience. And wi'out obedience the Jews, Moors and Freemasons'd swarm free, f' heretics breed like maggots on the decaying carcass o' the Church. All'll be ready on the day, Sire, on that burning Day o' Judgement when the good taste the greatest joy in Paradise—watching the torments o' the damned below—whilst the wicked see the terror awaiting 'em in Hell. Thus a successful auto de fe's both joy and terror mixed. A mighty show t' dazzle eyes and purge the heart; till that radiant moment when the Christian faith's made real and the playing ends and the last fires're lit and women roast and men burn t' hot ash, smoke in the wind. Oh there's nothing so inspiring, as sinners burning at the stake. It's good t' see 'em roasting, it's fine t' see 'em bake. The Jews'll shout 'Ovai, Ovai!', the Moors'll start t' quake. But their souls go marching on . . .

Whilst MONKS *enter and dismantle the set and the lights dim down,* VALLADARES *leads the* OTHERS *Down Stage singing ferociously to the painful, rhythmic cries of the* PRISONERS.

ALL (*singing*): We'll sing a holy chorus when they're screaming on the rack./We try to make them Christians but they all get cardiacs./We're rooting out the Devil and the other bric-a-brac./God is marching on./To keep the public happy is the object of the show./They need the entertainment and it helps the status quo./Men cannot live by bread alone . . .'

CARLOS (*singing*): 'But now we have to blow.'
ALL (*singing*): 'Cos the show is on the road./Glory, Glory Hallelujah./Glory, Glory Hallelujah./Glory, Glory Hallelujah./The show is on the road!'
  Lights out as they Exit.

SCENE XV

A single flute. Birds sing a dawn chorus. Misty morning light up on a bare bloodstained stage. A green and white Cross, both shrouded in black crepe Up Stage Left and Right. Running between them up to the Flies, three richly draped galleries. They become shorter in length the higher they are. Above the topmost gallery, a single box-platform with a rail. Two high ladders, Right and Left, link the galleries and platform. Below the bottom gallery a rostrum.

The birds stop singing as through the morning mist FOUR MONKS *of the Inquisition in conical hoods and black habits with white crosses on the front, enter silently, Stage Right, carrying wooden stakes. Another* MONK *enters behind them with a stoup and sprinkler. As the stakes are placed upright in a line Stage Right, he sprinkles each one in turn and blesses it. The 'Miserere' is chanted softly now and throughout the rest of the scene.*

Before the MONKS *exit they place steps Down Stage Centre to link the centre aisle of the auditorium to the Stage.*

There is a sound of crowds beginning to gather. PONTOCARRERO *in full cardinal's regalia, and* DR BRAVO *enter Down Stage Left each carrying a bundle of wood, as do* MOTILLA *and* ALMIRANTE, *who have entered Down Stage Right. Behind them, a silent line of* LADIES-IN-WAITING *and* COURTIERS *including* GONGORA, RAFAEL *and his father* MORRA, *each carrying a bundle of wood, make their way Up Stage and deposit their bundles at the foot of the stakes.*

Dividing into two snake-like lines they glide through the misty light and up the two gallery ladders Right and Left.

PONTOCARRERO: Observe His Majesty close. He's been poured into the tightest breeches so you canst see if his penis stands upright during the ceremony.

DR BRAVO: I fear his constitution's so weak 'twill be a miracle if *he* stands upright during the ceremony.

PONTOCARRERO: 'Tis the object o' the auto de fe t' work miracles.

The crowd grows louder now as the two lines of spectators climb up the gallery ladders.

MOTILLA: My lord, thy position's directly above the King so you canst observe if his penis-member grows apace.

ALMIRANTE: I dreamed only o' glory. Now my standard's in the dust, my honour's turned pimp.

MOTILLA: 'Twill be restored if after today's performance, the King performs between the sheets.

ALMIRANTE *and* MOTILLA, *together with* DR BRAVO *and* PONTOCARRERO, *join the end of the line of spectators and deposit their bundles of wood by the stakes.*

As the lights come up brighter and the crowd grows more excited, a PEDLAR *with a tray comes down the centre aisle of the auditorium.*

PEDLAR: Programmes! Official programmes from the Holy Office! Get your official programmes!

The COURTIERS *are now in place,* PONTOCARRERO *and* ALMIRANTE *in the lowest gallery.*

DR BRAVO *and a toothless* GONGORA *stand in position at the foot of the rostrum and glare at each other from opposite corners.* MOTILLA *Down Stage Centre faces them and the gallery.*

A drum-roll and the noise of the crowd instantly dies away and CARLOS *rises up from the back of the rostrum dressed completely in gold; even his face is painted gold. He is followed on either side by* ANA *and* MARIANA *in black, their faces chalk white. They take up*

positions; the women glaring viciously at each other, CARLOS
staring straight ahead.

*A pause, then the choir thunders the 'Miserere' and two purple
banners of the Inquisition unfurl from the Flies Up Stage Left and
Right behind the Crosses. At the same time* VALLADARES, *accompanied by the* EXECUTIONER *in tight-fitting black hood and
trousers and a fiery cross burnt on his chest, appears on the platform
above the gallery.*

The stiff brocade of VALLADARES' *pontificals spread out over
the edge of the platform making him look like a purple bat hovering
in the air.*

As VALLADARES *delivers the sermon the* EXECUTIONER *very
slowly slides down the gallery ladder.*

VALLADARES: 'Beautiful art thou my beloved like the skins o'
Solomon.' Thus the Holy Ghost likened the Church t' the
tents o' the Israelites adorned in the skins o' the wild beasts
they'd slain. So the Holy Inquisition's most beautiful, adorned
wi' the skins o' God's enemies she too hath slain. Some will die
reconciled in the true Faith, others remaining obstinate t' the
last. Both fall. But the good die falling forward like Abraham,
t'wards God, the wicked backwards, away into Hell. Grant us
thy mercy, Lord.

The crowd chants 'Amen' and TWO MONKS *enter Stage Left
bearing a huge Bible. One crouches in front of the rostrum whilst the*
OTHER *opens the Bible and rests it on his back whilst* MOTILLA
intones above.

MOTILLA: Your Majesty swears and promises by thy faith
and royal word thou wilt defend the Catholic Faith which
you do hold and believe. That you will persecute the heretic
and apostate against our Holy Mother the Apostolic Church o'
Rome according t' the decrees and sacred laws wi'out omission
or exception.

CARLOS: This do I swear and promise by my faith and royal
word.

The crowd chants 'Amen'. As the Bible is carried out Stage Left

MOTILLA *moves Up Stage towards the rostrum, bows deeply, turns and faces the auditorium. A* MONK *stands on either side of him, one with the sentences of the accused, the other with a white cord on a small black cushion. Behind them the* COURTIERS *shift expectantly.*

A funeral bell tolls as a candle-lit procession comes down the centre aisle of the auditorium. Flanked by black-hooded MONKS, *both live and dead* CRIMINALS *wear white, penitent cloaks called 'Sarbenitos' and tall, cone-shaped dunce's caps; flames decorate the cloaks and the hats of those about to be burnt. Each* CRIMINAL *carries a lighted yellow candle and they have their names scrawled on placards on their chests.*

A PRIEST, *carrying the Cross of St Martin veiled in black, leads them in. In order behind him are* LEONORA SANCHEZ, *her neck in a knotted yoke, her torn dress bespattered with mud;* JUAN *and* LUCIA GUZMAN, *half-dead in their chains; the smouldering skeleton of* NUNO ALVAREZ *in the tattered remains of a shroud,* LOPEZ DURO, *gagged and manacled, his hat painted with dragons as well as flames; and the life-size wax effigy of* GREGORIO MADERA *on a litter with a Janus mask on the front and back of its head.*

As they stagger down amid the incessant chanting and the jeers and catcalls of the crowd, two PEDLARS *with trays make their way up side aisles, one crying* 'Hot chocolate! Sweet cakes! Get thy hot chocolate!' *and the other* 'Souvenirs! Crucifixes! Beads! Virgin Marys! Authentic splinters from the stakes! Only two ducats.'

The PRIEST *at the head of the procession, climbs up onto the Stage, where all bow their heads before the Cross of St Martin. As he solemnly exits with it Stage Left,* MOTILLA *begins flatly to read out the sentences. The instant the condemned* CRIMINALS *step up onto the Stage before him, their candles are snuffed out.*

MOTILLA: This is the first group o' criminal penitents, consigned t' judgement . . . Accursed limb o' Satan, Leonora Sanchez, widow o' Nicholas Sanchez, guilty o' bigamy, abandoned t' the secular arm and sentenced t' one hundred lashes in a

public street according t' custon wi'out mercy or remission.
*To the jeers of the crowd the hysterical woman is dragged Off
Stage Left accompanied by a* PRIEST.

PRIEST: Repent my daughter. Search thy heart. Confess thy
sins. Ask God's forgiveness afore 'tis too late.

MOTILLA: Accursed limbs o' Satan, Juan and Lucia Guzman,
found guilty o' a heretical proposition concerning self-
damnation. Thou hast adjured, confessed thy errors, been
reconciled and sentenced t' be abandoned t' the secular arm
and executed according t' custom, wi'out mercy or remission.

A MONK *takes the half-dead* GUZMANS *to the* EXECUTIONER
and the stakes, Stage Right, accompanied by the PRIEST *who has
quickly returned.*

PRIEST: Repent, my children. Search thy hearts. Confess thy
sins. Ask God's forgiveness afore 'tis too late.

As the EXECUTIONER *binds the* GUZMANS *to separate stakes
and the sound of* LEONORA SANCHEZ *being whipped Off Stage
Left is heard,* ALMIRANTE *quickly produces a telescope, claps it
to his eye and focuses on* CARLOS's *crotch directly below him.*

MOTILLA: Accursed limb o' Satan, Nuno Alvarez 1564–1638.
Found guilty and sentenced f' secret Protestantism. The lands
o' thy descendants to be confiscated and thy bones disinterred
and taken t' the place o' burning and abandoned t' the secular
arm according t' custom wi'out mercy or remission.

The skeleton of ALVAREZ *is carried Stage Right with the*
PRIEST *fervently exhorting the bones.*

PRIEST: Repent, my son. Search thy heart. Confess thy sins.
Ask God's forgiveness afore 'tis too late.

As the EXECUTIONER *binds the skeleton to a stake,* DR BRAVO
*is seen taking out a large magnifying glass and shifting to a better
position to peer up* CARLOS's *crotch directly above him.*

Amid the incessant noise and lights the crowd shouts excitedly as
LOPEZ DURO *approaches* MOTILLA.

MOTILLA: Accursed limb o' Satan, Lopez Duro, guilty o'
Judaism and who, despite the ministerings o' the Holy Office

remains a pertinacious, unreconciled heretic. Sentenced t' be abandoned t' the secular arm f' burning according to custom wi'out mercy or remission.

DURO *looks up at* VALLADARES *and nods. Imperceptibly* VALLADARES *nods back.* DURO *is led away Stage Right savagely kicking the accompanying* PRIEST *about the shins.*

PRIEST: Repent, my son *ahhh*. Search thy . . . *ahh ahh* . . . confess *ahh* . . . (*Quickly*.) Ask-God's-forgiveness-afore-'tis-too-late *aaahhh*.

The crowd bays loudly as DURO *is tied to a stake.*

The whippings, the unending chanting of the 'Miserere' and the fierce unrelenting light have an hypnotic effect. MOTILLA's *voice becomes inaudible as he passes sentence on the wax effigy.*

MOTILLA: Accursed limb o' Satan, Gregorio Madera, guilty in absentis o' extreme Mohammedanism . . . sentenced . . . 'in absentis' . . . confiscation . . . effigy taken . . . abandoned . . . burning . . .

He continues speaking but his words are drowned out. So are the PRIEST's *accompanying the effigy as it is taken Stage Right.*

Amid thunderous chants the EXECUTIONER *binds the effigy to the stake furthest Down Stage Right, crosses Stage Centre and faces the spectators in the galleries, some of whom have been bored by the preceding ceremony. The* MONK *with the white cord on the cushion steps towards him. Taking the cord the* EXECUTIONER *holds it up high to* VALLADARES *who makes the sign of the Cross and blesses it.*

Lights begin to dim down and the noise dies away to a soft chanting. A single bell tolls as the EXECUTIONER *crosses back Stage Right. The spectators in the galleries lean forward, trembling with excitement.* DR BRAVO *and* ALMIRANTE *even stop watching* CARLOS's *crotch and* ANA *and* MARIANA, *each other.*

The EXECUTIONER *stops in front of the terrified* LEONORA GUZMAN *tied to the Up Stage stake. Silence now except for the crowd's excited breathing. Even that ceases suddenly as the* EXECUTIONER *in one swift movement, loops the cord round*

LEONORA's *neck and pulls tight. There is a hoarse 'Uggh' and she sags forward, garotted. The crowd roars 'Olé'.*

The single bell tolls and the EXECUTIONER *moves down to* JUAN GUZMAN. *Silence, then the same swift movement with the cord, a strangled 'Uggh' and the crowd roaring 'Olé'.*

As the bell begins tolling ominously again a LADY-IN-WAITING *falls out of the lower gallery, laughing wildly, in a fit of hysteria. No one pays any attention. They are too busy watching the* EXECUTIONER *in front of the skeleton of* ALVAREZ. *Again silence and the swift movement of the cord around the victim's neck. But this time no 'Uggh' but a sharp 'crack' of bone. The crowd roars 'Olé'.*

The light is now dim. A hooded MONK *enters Stage Right with a lighted rush-torch and hands it to the* EXECUTIONER. *The bell tolls above the choir and noise of the crowd as he solemnly lights the Up Stage stake. He then proceeds down the line lighting each stake in turn, ending with the one bearing* MADERA's *wax effigy.*

The stage is now dark except for Spots on the figures of VALLADARES *suspended high in the darkness and* CARLOS *on the rostrum below him. Stage Right the stakes form a seeming endless row of glowing, red lights stretching away into the night. The dim shape of* DURO *can be vaguely glimpsed writhing in agony but we can only clearly see* MADERA's *wax effigy Down Stage, quickly melting under the heat.*

As the red wax bubbles and flows like blood, CARLOS *shifts position, legs apart. A monstrous phallus sprouts from between them. The choir bursts forth triumphantly singing* 'Hallelujah! Hallelujah! Hallelujah! The strife is o'er, the battle done . . .' *as the enormous phallus grows to become a massive eight feet long, and two feet thick.*

When it overhangs the edge of the rostrum a PRIEST *emerges from out of the darkness, bends under it and lifts it on his shoulders. As he helps* CARLOS *and his phallus manoeuvre their way off the rostrum,* ANA *emerges Down Stage Left, in a nightdress and the choir sings,* 'Now the victor's triumph won, O let the song o' praise be sung. Hallelujah . . !' CARLOS *and his giant phallus come down off the rostrum to meet her.*

The light on VALLADARES *fades but the long line of stakes continues to glow. As the effigy's limbs blister, melt and slide off, the* MONK *moves away into the darkness and* CARLOS *turns to face* ANA *holding up his phallus on his own.*

The choir sings 'Hallelujah, Hallelujah, Hallelujah!' *They move towards each other and* ANA *is impaled on the tip of the colossal phallus. Clinging to it, she is lifted off her feet and borne backwards whilst the voices soar:* 'Death's mightiest powers have done their worst, and Jesus hath his foes dispersed; Let shouts of praise and joy outburst . . .'

The fires glow, MADERA's *wax effigy finally buckles and dissolves and* ANA *vanishes into the Wings riding* CARLOS's *rearing phallus to a mighty* 'Hallelujah! Hallelujah! Hallelujah!'

END OF ACT ONE

ACT TWO

SCENE I

Spot Down Stage Centre on the PARROT *on its perch.*

PARROT: *O impotence, where is thy sting? Nothing's changed. Carlos sits i' the dust anointing his penis-stick wi' goat's grease and the Queen's still barren, CRRAH CRRAH. So what else's new? Barcelona's still besieged by the French, and the poor still starve. Men don't get results, only consequences. The Court's turned henhouse, the Queen Mother's triumphed. She holds the country in the hollow o' her head. CRRAH CRRAH . . .*
    MARIANA *appears in the Spot behind the bird.*
Joey's flight's flown. She's come t' kill me. What matter. Death holds no terrors. I'll fly the Northern passage to the sun and dream dim parrot-dreams o' everlasting jungles. My parrot soul goes up into sunlight t' join the celestial company o' parrots and perch afore the one true Parrot-God, the almighty Psittacidae, our Creator and Judge, the Great Beak Himself, CRRAH, OH CRRAH.
    MARIANA *picks up the perch and* PARROT *and disappears with it into the darkness Stage Left.*
Goodnight Joey, poor Joey—a bird like me comes once every hundred years. (singing) *'Come fly wi' me, come fly away t' some . . . ARWK'.*
    A final strangulated squawk, silence.

SCENE II

CARLOS's *terrified cries in the darkness. Lights up on the King's Bedchamber, with the fourposter Stage Left, below it a small table with a white cloth, crucifix, cotton wool, bread towel and bowl. Double door Up Stage Centre and the skeleton of Saint Isidore on his bier in front of the mirror Stage Right.*

A sick, trembling CARLOS *lies propped up on a cushion in an armchair Stage Centre. He has a dead pigeon tied on the top of his head, two black leeches on his face and his bare foot rests in a basin.* DR BRAVO *is bleeding his big toe.* RAFAEL *watches* DR GELEEN *pour a yellow medicine from the medical cabinet into a glass whilst* MARIANA *and* PONTOCARRERO *consult some documents and* GONGORA *looks over his astrological charts.*

Sobbing in pain, CARLOS *tugs feebly at* DR BRAVO *as he examines his blood in the basin.*

CARLOS: Saa saaaave eeeee. I'm at death's door.

DR BRAVO: Ne'er fear, Sire, I'll pull you through. (*Sniffs blood.*) Black bile, true melancholic blood. Doest have pain passing water?

RAFAEL: No, but he gets giddy crossing a bridge.

DR BRAVO: The dead pigeon 'll prevent any more such attacks o' vertigo. (*Pulls off leeches.*) Sire, I believe thine's a hard case o' tertian fever, complicated by bone-ache, gut-grip and *rheums*. But Medicine's a science o' probability and uncertainty.

RAFAEL: Certainly the way you practise it.

GONGORA: The moon's in Leo, and Leo and the 5th House reign o'er the heart, liver, stomach and left papp. But now the moon's free from the lord o' the 6th and 8th House, *salutem significat*. This foretells life, Sire, and good recovery.

DR BRAVO: You also foretold a good pregnancy and a successful auto de fe.

GONGORA: God willed a sudden star-change.

RAFAEL: Don't tell us o' your failures, your successes're depressing enough.

GONGORA: Doctor, thy own star-course hasn't changed. At the time o' the square o' the progressed Uranus t' the Moon, prepare f' death.

   DR BRAVO *scowls and gives* CARLOS *the yellow medicine which he shakily drinks.*

MARIANA (*puts documents on* CARLOS's *lap*): Son, sign these and rest. They make me Queen Regent, His Eminence First Minister, and José o' Bavaria heir t' the throne.

   CARLOS *nods.* PONTOCARRERO *holds the quill and ink-horn in front of him. With a great effort* CARLOS *picks up the quill, leans forward to sign and vomits up the yellow medicine over the papers.* PONTOCARRERO *quickly snatches them away, but they are soaked.*

   He and MARIANA *control their frustration and try to dry them whilst* DR BRAVO *thrusts the basin onto* CARLOS's *lap.*

DR BRAVO: Cascade free, Sire, thy victualling stomach's fever-clogged. This saffron and thassia-root emetic'll clear 't out afore I administer the licorice purge. I want you cascading at both ends.

RAFAEL: You've no need o' emetics t' make you vomit, Sire. Jus' look around you.

   BELEPSCH *enters urgently Up Stage pushing* ANA *in a wheel chair, trembling with fever and wrapped in blankets.* MOTILLA *accompanies them, carrying a covered silver dinner-tray.*

DR BRAVO: Your Majesty, this is unwise! Movement only inflames feverish blood. The cure's resting, bleeding and a lenten diet o' black cherry-water, egg yolks and breast o' boiled fowl ...

ANA: Then how was I served *this*?

   MOTILLA *uncovers the dish to reveal the carcass of Joey the* PARROT. DR BRAVO *examines it gravely.*

DR BRAVO: No, that's not suitable. Why, 'tisn't even plucked.

ANA: Plucked? Plucked? The fowl's dead, foully murdered! 'Tis my Joey, my Joey!

GONGORA: Saturn's in the 12th House, Your Majesty; plots, betrayals, assaults i' the dark. 'Tis how I came t' lose my teeth.

RAFAEL (*saluting with flask*): Alas, poor Joey. Thy loon's licence hast been revoked, *Crrah Crrah*.

ANA: Help me, Carlos, help me! Joey's the only thing I e'er loved. I know WHO, Madame . . . I know . . .

MARIANA: I glory in 't. I'd meant t' turn cook and serve him baked; wrapped in light pastry, hot parrot-pie à la Mariana. (*Chanting*.) 'And when the pie was opened the parrot couldn't sing. Oh wasn't that a dainty dish t' set afore a Queen.'

CARLOS (*retching*): Uggghh.

ANA: I'll see thee crap'd and dangled in gallows air f' this! (*She staggers up.*) Kill! Kill! Kill! *Ahhh.* (*She slumps back.*)

BELEPSCH: Quick, quick! Der Tod . . . she's dying.

DR BRAVO *makes* ANA *drink the remains of* CARLOS's *emetic.*

PONTOCARRERO: Return Her Majesty t' her chambers.

MARIANA: No, if she's dying let her stay so's I canst see her death and she my triumph!

ANA *seated opposite* CARLOS *vomits into the basin that has been placed in her lap. Both she and* CARLOS *retch repeatedly as* DR BRAVO *hurries between them with more emetic to drink.*

PONTOCARRERO: Not thy triumph, Ma'am, but the triumph o' moderation. Only patience and experience'll keep the nation and Empire intact. These proclamations can mark a historic return t' stability and order.

He places the documents before CARLOS *who, with a tremendous effort, signs the top one.* MARIANA *snatches it away before he can vomit over it.*

CARLOS *sinks back, too exhausted to continue for the moment.*

MARIANA (*breathing deeply*): *Haaa* . . . I can BREATHE again. I've reached the mountain peak. (*She waves the document at* ANA.) *Crrah. Crrah.* I'm Regent, Madame. You lost 't all i' that barren bed. Go die in thy own vomit. My son's returned t' me and his power . . . Haaa, I've climbed up o'er my pain. My will alone, Madame, my WILL. Now's all easy and relaxed.

I canst do what . . . do anything . . . do everything . . . What do y' want t' do . . .? What . . .? It snaps back round my throat . . . a thousand fissures . . . soft cavities appear . . . suddenly sag . . . 'tis too easy . . . Aie. Aie. Ai . . . (*She falters as she alone sees the* OLD MAN *from Act I, Scene III, come down out of the curtained bed where he has been hiding and hobble towards her.*) AIE . . . Not me . . . HER . . . *AIEEEEE*.

   She cries with pain as a knife flashes and he stabs her in the chest above her crab brooch. DR BRAVO *catches her as she falls backwards and the* OLD MAN *exits chuckling.*

DR BRAVO: Quick, t' the bed.

   DR GELEEN *helps carry* MARIANA *to the bed.*

PONTOCARRERO: What struck her?

GONGORA: The malefics Mars and Saturn.

BELEPSCH: Where?! Where?! I didst not see 'em.

   ANA *and* CARLOS *still retch violently as* MARIANA *is laid on the bed and* DR BRAVO *whispers to* DR GELEEN *who hurries out.*

DR BRAVO: 'Tis what we afeared when we examined her last. Your Majesties, the Queen Mother's suffering from what my famed colleague Cornelius Celsus called a carcinoma or cancer o' the breast.

PONTOCARRERO: 'Carcinoma', 'cancer'? Why wasn't I told?

DR BRAVO: Wishing t' spare you, she swore us t' secrecy.

GONGORA: She swore me, too, when I discovered Cancer 'd entered the 4th House.

PONTOCARRERO: And left this one blasted. He casn't take her from me now. Barcelona's besieged, our armies slow-starving. My work's not done. Re-consider, Ma'am!

MOTILLA: God's wrath falls on the children o' disobedience.

PONTOCARRERO: Call her back. Leech her. Drain her!

DR BRAVO: Blood letting's contra-indicated. Only attenuant and evacuant medicine can be used.

RAFAEL: Keep politics out o' this.

PONTOCARRERO: What o' me? What o' the succession? What o' Spain?

DR BRAVO: Her tumour's the size o' the head o' a seven-year-old child but leathery, overgrown wi' fungus. The carcinoma spreads daily, eating her alive. Morte morieris. She's endured terrible suffering, 'tis a wonder she was able t' stand upright. But even great oaks fall at the last . . .

RAFAEL (*softly*): T-i-m-b-e-r.

CARLOS *gives an incoherent cry of despair, leaps up panic-stricken, stumbles over to his Mother, trips and sends the contents of the basin over the bed. He flaps his arms helplessly as* MARIANA, *still clutching the proclamation, struggles amid the soiled bedclothes.*

MARIANA: I couldst've ruled like a lion. Now I die like a dog. Why shouldst I die? He who loses his life f' Christ shall find 't. But not yet, Lord. NOT YET. Let me breathe, then I'll gladly putrefy. But not now, Lord, NOT NOW . . . (*A choir sings softly Psalm 29: 'De profundis clamo ad te'.*) 'Tis a time t' cast up accounts. My sins 're great I confess, but I flee t' God's mercy . . . Son . . . daughter . . . come close . . .

BELEPSCH *helps* ANA *to stagger up and join* CARLOS, *on his knees by the bed. The* OTHERS *bow their heads and the choir chants softly.*

Let's exchange forgiveness. Ana, I persecuted thee f' stealing my son from me. Carlos, I wounded thee, too, out o' love. Alas, only God can wound us into 't. Carlos . . . Carlos . . . list, list. There's no wisdom i' the grave. Make the symbol o' thy authority the olive branch, not the gallows tree, not the cold sword but the warm heart. Oh let love flow out like honey and balm, wine and sweetwater. Oh children, Jesus hath written us in his hand, now write him lovingly in thy HEARTS!

ANA ⎱
CARLOS ⎰ : *Ugggg!*

Unable to stop themselves, they both vomit over MARIANA. BELEPSCH *and* RAFAEL *rush to* ANA *and* CARLOS *respectively whilst* GONGORA *studies his charts and* MOTILLA *helps* PONTOCARRERO *prepare 'Extreme Unction' at the table.*

As the sodden figure of MARIANA *thrashes about wildly in fear and craws hoarsely,* CARLOS *suddenly staggers over to the skeleton.*

CARLOS: Maaamaa, the ddddancing BONES o' Saint Isidore aaaaa the Crucifix o' the Holy Father mamamaa (*Clutching the skeleton and crucifix he carries them back to the bed.*) Work miracles . . . DANCE damn yooo DANCE . . .

Whilst he rattles the skeleton furiously, ANA *and* BELEPSCH *try to prise the proclamation from* MARIANA'*s clenched fist.*

They tear half of it away as MARIANA *screams and struggles with* DR BRAVO, *bringing down the bed curtains in her frenzy.* CARLOS *throws the skeleton on the bed and waves the crucifix over her helplessly.*

PONTOCARRERO: Be not taken wild, Ma'am. You didst not live pale, do not die trembling. Death should've a dignity!

ANA: I suddenly feel better. Thanks be t' God.

PONTOCARRERO (*chanting*): 'Adiutorum nostrum . . .'

CARLOS *collapses sobbing on the floor, and* RAFAEL *tries to comfort him.* DR BRAVO *restrains the hysterical* MARIANA *as* PONTOCARRERO *gloomily approaches with the oil of the sick in a bowl, accompanied by a delighted* MOTILLA *acting as server with pieces of wool and bread on a gold plate.*

PONTOCARRERO *dips his right thumb into the oil and makes a cross with it on* MARIANA'*s wet forehead.*

PONTOCARRERO (*chanting*): 'Per istam sanctam Unctionem, indulget tibi Dominus quidquid deliquista. Amen.'

Even as MOTILLA *wipes away the oil with the wool and* PONTOCARRERO *dries his thumb on the bread,* MARIANA *blindly lashes out and knocks the bowl of oil out of his hand and over herself and the bed.*

All struggle to hold her down, but now covered with oil she slips from their grasp.

MARIANA: Let me breathe!

ANA: Gi' me the proclamation—then go die!

MOTILLA: See God's mercy, wonderful t' behold!

GONGORA: 'Tis the malefics, the naughty malefics!

B—4*

He tries to show them his charts but they fall out of his hands and he becomes involved in a messy scramble with PONTOCARRERO *trying to retrieve the bowl and* BELEPSCH *and* ANA *the proclamation. During it, the skeleton of St Isidore is flung off the bed and lands on top of* CARLOS *who is pinned to the ground gibbering with fear.*

As RAFAEL *pulls off the greasy bones, the bespattered* MARIANA *suddenly tears herself free from the scrummage and staggers upright on the sodden bed, gasping ferociously for breath whilst the lights dim down.*

MARIANA: *Haaa . . . haaa . . .* the light . . . the light . . . See, see 't falls . . .! (*She points up as the roof of the four-poster bed slowly descends.*) God 've mercy, Holy Mother . . . let me exchange eternal life in paradise f' one more hour o' pain . . . see, see 't falls . . .! (*She topples backwards as the top of the bed sinks lower and we can see in the increasing gloom it is the lid of an ornamental sarcophagus.*) Death's 'tween my thighs . . . feet press me down . . . *haaa . . .* Lord My Redeemer Saviour Christ, I hurt, I hurt, therefore I am, I am!

The sarcophagus descends on her. A great stony thud reverberates endlessly as the top falls into place in the darkness. Silence.

CARLOS: *Mamaaaaaaa.*

SCENE III

A funeral bell tolls, the 'Miserere' is sung and four PRIESTS *with black candles enter Up Stage Centre; behind them a line of mourning* COURTIERS.

Crossing Stage Left, in flickering light, they attach the candles to the four corners of the sarcophagus which is then carried slowly Stage Right whilst the MOURNERS *march solemnly behind and* PONTO-CARRERO *is heard intoning the funeral oration.*

PONTOCARRERO: Death's not everlasting Night, but everlasting Light. There's a mercy in every malediction, a Resurrection in every last end. God's now pity-bound t' recompense us f' the loss o' our Watchtower, our Nurse, our beloved Queen Mother, Doña Mariana, by gi'ing Spain an heir. She was cast down that this nation couldst be delivered up from its enemies. Bow knee and neck, redemption draws nigh!

The candles are snuffed out and the MOURNERS *exit Up Stage Centre.*

As the singing dies, pale, dusty lights come up on the Royal Vault. A small iron gate Up Stage Centre with steps leading up beyond it. Stage Right and Left, a wall niche decorated with a pyramid of human skulls surmounted by a Cross.

CARLOS *crouches by the sarcophagus and* ANA *stands beside him with a loaf of bread and flask of wine. They speak in whispers throughout.*

ANA: Fifty thousand masses're being said and twelve candles lit in every church in Spain f' the Seven Works o' Mercy and the Five Wounds o' Christ. What more canst we do f' the repose o' her Soul?

CARLOS: Die.

ANA: I miss her too. Hate was a cloak, kept me warm nights. She leaves a gap. We'll fill 't wi' each other. (*Gives him wine and bread.*) Eat, drink, Carlos.

CARLOS (*eating and drinking*): The bbbread's stale, wine's sour.

ANA (*wiping wine from his doublet*): Come back up wi' me, Carlos. Now she's not standing betwixt us, we'll do things together.

CARLOS: TTTooo-ther? Whaaa thii . . .?

ANA: Whatever people do together.

CARLOS: IIIII'm not *people*.

ANA: We couldst play spillikins together. Or skittle pool, dice or hazard. Yes, we couldst play hazard together. (*She gives him a pack of cards which immediately cascade out of his hands.*) Well, then, we couldst dance together: Pavan, Courante, Gavotte. Yes, we couldst dance the Gavotte together. (*She pulls him up to perform a few steps but he quickly becomes entangled in his own feet.*) Well, then, we couldst jus' touch hands, fingers, lips i' a kiss: (*he goes to kiss her mouth, misses and ends up biting her left ear: she sings softly.*) 'Lucky in love, no I never will be lucky in love/Gay times are few, few skies are blue./Good luck scattered when I first looked at you./(CARLOS *accompanies her in a quiet adenoidal screech.*) We don't know what the future will bring/But if we're together, it won't mean a thing . . .'

CARLOS: 'That's certain.'

ANA (*moving Up Stage, singing*): 'Lucky in love, must be fun t' be someone,/Who's Oh so lucky in love.' (*She stops by the small gate.*) Joey's dead, Carlos. Come up wi' me . . . (CARLOS *hesitates.*) I'll go count gold and silver then. (*The gate shuts behind her with a clang as she exits up the vault steps.*) Sweet Jesu, gi' me someone t' hate! Sweet Jesu, someone t' hate!

As he finally starts after her the sarcophagus lid opens slightly and a skeleton hand shoots out, grabbing his shoulder.

CARLOS: *Mama.* (*He tries to move away.*) *Aaaaaaa.* (*He is pulled back.*) *Maamaaa.* (*He struggles to free himself as lights dim down to a Spot.*) *Maaamaaaa . . . maaaa . . . aaa . . . maa . . aa . . aa . . .* (*The Spot flickers and his struggle turns into an epileptic seizure, legs and arms splaying grotesquely, his whole body convulsed. He seems about to fall, but the skeleton hand repeatedly jerks him upright. His wild gyrations quickly die down and in a state of post-epileptic automation he whispers into the sarcophagus.*) Mama. Mama. 'Tis hard t' lose a Mother . . . (*Simulating* MARIANA's *voice.*) *Almost impossible, son.* Where're you, Mother? *Somewhere i' the distant gong.* Are you dead, Mama? *Dead t' the world, alive wi' white sluggies. I think, therefore I am. I stink, therefore I am not.* Mama, canst hear the flowers grow and the silent lobster scuttle past? *I can hear my bones creak, flesh drip, drip, drip away.* Mama, art still Queen? *Queen o' worms, shadows, dirt and dungheaps.* What's the meaning o' life, Mama? *T' keep one's balance, wings're best.* Help me Mama. God gave me crown, sceptre, throne: as he reigns

in the heaven so I reign on earth. I stretch out my hand t'
bring order t' the Universe. But Mama, t' has no edge, no
bottom, no centre, no 'now', 'before' or 'after'; one thing
doesn't lead t' another, time contracts, stones die and the
apple doesn't fall, the earth rushes up t' meet 't. There'er no
parallels t' a given line through a given point—or millions
o' 'em. What's the true geometry, Mama, when all possi-
bilities're equally consistent? How can I rule when God's gi'en
up the ghost? What chance've I when He's left all things t'
take their chances? I flounder, Mama. Help me rule, Mama.
Tell me the secret. I'll be your little boy again, hurt only
you, Mama. Tell me the secret . . . Whisper 't me . . . I'll come
closer, Mama . . . closer . . .

*As he slides into the sarcophagus his Spot fades out, leaving only
the Spot on the empty throne and whispers in the darkness.*

SCENE IV

*The whispering grows louder like the sound of thousands of insects.
Lights slowly up on the Throne Room where* RAFAEL *sits on the
edge of the throne watching* ALBA, TORRES *and* MONTERREY
scuttle about, whispering furiously, as ALMIRANTE *enters Stage
Left with papers and an* ATTENDANT. *They turn to him. The
sound stops instantly.*

ALMIRANTE: My lords, Barcelona's fallen t' the French.
TORRES: Hannibal ad portas. 'Tis the end! My books!
MONTERREY: My Government bonds! 'Tis the dark night o'
the soul. This's a defeat as great as Algeria's.
ALMIRANTE: Is 't? (*He gives papers to the* ATTENDANT, *who
exits.*) When an army's truly defeated? 'Tis difficult t' say, my
lord. Men're easily replaced, ground retaken. Who's defeated
's a matter o' opinion. I throw my men twixt your two

armies and cry 'I've split 'em, you're lost!' You shout, 'You've put yourself 'tween two fires, *you're* lost!' The defeats o' history only happened when one commander believed himself defeated, whereas in the same circumstances, wi' exactly the same losses, another would've 'Te Deums' sung and bells rung t' proclaim a great victory. And 'cause he believed 't, that credulous whore, history'd believe 't too. I'll ne'er be defeated, my lords. Rest easy. The Queen's gi'en me command o' a new army. The French're now trapped in Barcelona, their lines extended, their strength exhausted. They're ripe f' plucking. We should gi' thanks t' God f' this triumph

MONTERREY: 'Tis true, victory, like money's a matter of confidence; 't goes t' them that have 't.

ALBA: Blood must triumph!

ALMIRANTE: Reality's a crutch f' the common people!

TORRES: We'll sweep 'em back t' Paris which we'll fire, scatter, plough and salt! Delendam esse Carthaginem. Delendam esse Carthaginem.

ALBA: And when they sue f' peace we'll demand Luxembourg, Santo Domingo, Antilles and French Guinea f' the Crown.

MONTERREY: Guinea? Let 'em keep that rat-infested plague isle, we'll seize sugar-sweet Tobago 'stead o' Guinea.

ALBA: Tobago?! Tobago's nothing! Spain must have Guinea; 'tis where the cocoa nuts come from.

ALMIRANTE: We'll annexe both Tobago *and* Guinea. T' the victor the spoils!

RAFAEL: Gi' us another victory like Barcelona and we'll be on our knees begging f' mercy. Does the King know o' this 'victory'?

ALMIRANTE: No, thanks t' your incompetence, Master Zany, he's still entombed wi' the dead. 'Tis your duty t' laugh him out o' his black humour. When a performing flea fails his master, he's dismissed . . . (*Claps hands together.*) 'squashed flea'. Careful thou doestn't become 'squashed Zany'.

RAFAEL: Is 't true, my lord, you're so witless, if your brain had a thought it'd die o' loneliness?

ALMIRANTE: Is 't true you're so small a pigeon perched on thy shoulder can pick a pea out your arse?

RAFAEL (*crosses to him, bows and kicks him on the shins*): I Rafael Morra, Court Jester to His Majesty, Carlos o' Spain, formally challenge you.

ALMIRANTE (*laughing*): Spindle Shanks, you've not the pedigree, title or height t' challenge a grandee. Go challenge thy superiors, the nits, gnats and gnomes. I've a nation t' save.

RAFAEL: White-livered gullion! I expected you t' slink away wi' your tail 'tween your legs and the Queen's!

ALMIRANTE (*drawing sword*): SIR.

RAFAEL (*drawing tiny sword*): SIR.

An ATTENDANT *enters Stage Right.*

ATTENDANT: My lords, Her Most Gracious Majesty, Queen Ana o' Spain.

ANA *enters carrying the dead* PARROT, *stuffed and stuck on a short perch, and accompanied by* BELEPSCH *and* MOTILLA. *All bow.*

ANA: My lord Alba, what a beautiful pendant you wear.

ALBA (*grudgingly*): Please accept 't as a token o' my love f' Your Majesty's person.

ANA: Oh, isn't that most gallant, Joey? (*The* PARROT *falls sideways.*) We graciously accept thy gift, my lord. (*As* ALBA *takes off the pendant and drops it into a black bag* BELEPSCH *holds open for him,* ANA *passes on to* TORRES *and gestures to the book he is holding:* TORRES *forces a smile and gives it to her.*) Vellum. We graciously accept thy gift, my lord. (*She drops the book into the bag.*) My brother informs me he's taken t' collecting rare books. I believe your library's the best in Spain. Joey and I propose t' honour you wi' a visit after Lent. (TORRES *gives a horrified cry and sways, but* ANA *passes on unconcerned to* MONTERREY, *who has already taken off a sapphire ring and dropped it, with a sigh, into the bag.*) We graciously accept thy gift: examine 't close, Countess, my lord Monterrey's taken t' wearing paste in my presence.

RAFAEL: What gift canst I gi' t' please Your Majesty?

ANA: Your *tongue*—by the roots. (*She crosses and sits on the throne.*) Joey, even stuffed you're more alive than these grandees.

MOTILLA: My lords, the Queen on behalf o' His Majesty and i' accordance wi' his wishes decrees His Eminence the Cardinal-Archbishop o' Toledo be banished from Madrid and I take his place on the Council o' State. And further, the Archduke Charles o' Austria be declared heir t' the throne. Do you so agree? (*They all raise their hands.*) Now Spain can rise again. Now like Peter the Hermit I can go preach a Holy Crusade 'gainst the infidel Louis and stained in the wine-press o' the Lord, wade ankle-deep through his blood t' salvation . . . (*Lights dim down.*) Now, wi' the new army we'll fight i' the light o' faith, the light that pierces, God's light, condensed sunlight.

ALMIRANTE: Rejoice. Madrid celebrates the victorious fall o' Barcelona!

ANA: Rejoice. Let the righteous rejoice wi' Jerusalem. We're His again!

BELEPSCH: Rejoice. God, Thy arm was there. 'Tis Thy victory!

MOTILLA: Rejoice. He hath brought His people from the depths that their feet may be dipped in their enemies' blood! 'Tis my victory!

Bells peal, the 'Te Deum' is sung and LADIES-IN-WAITING *enter Right and Left with lighted sparklers.*

Led by the QUEEN, *and holding a sparkler each, all dance joyfully in the darkness.*

The sparklers finally splutter out and they all exit except MOTILLA *who stands Up Stage Centre smiling triumphantly in a solitary light. It dies out with the 'Te Deum'.*

Lights up on PONTOCARRERO's *Chamber with doors Stage Right and Up Stage Centre. Most of the rich furnishings have been removed though there are still deep red drapes on the walls.*

TWO JESUIT PRIESTS *systematically carry out Stage Right, rolled carpets, paintings, silverware and personal belongings whilst* FROYLAN *and* PONTOCARRERO *check through bundles of State papers on the floor Down Stage Right. They do not notice* MOTILLA *watching them in the shadows by the door Up Stage Centre.*

PONTOCARRERO: Careful wi' that painting, Father, 'twas gi'en me by Diego de Silva himself. If the forty pack-horses don't suffice, hire more and double-arm the escorts in case o' bandits. At least I'll have my goods about me while I'm rotting back in Toledo . . . (*Shudders.*) *Toledo*, I tell you that city's a cemetery wi' lights!

FROYLAN: But you're Cardinal-Archbishop o' Toledo, Your Eminence.

PONTOCARRERO: Someone had t' be. I lost.

FROYLAN: But Toledo has a great tradition o' necromancy. Once men skilled i' the magic arts publicly taught pyromancy, geomancy and e'en hydromancy. I confess I look forward t' continuing my researches there. I hope t' catch me a strix. That's a rare sorceress who cries like a screech-owl, *eeeaaa eeeaaa.*

PONTOCARRERO: I'd rather be dead in Madrid than alive in Toledo.

MOTILLA: That too can be arranged, Your Eminence, if you stay here. Remember my tolerance begins only where my power ends.

As he crosses Down Stage, FROYLAN *bows and helps the* PRIESTS *remove* PONTOCARRERO's *belongings.*

PONTOCARRERO: The Queen Mother's death's sent you t' the top o' fortune's wheel. But take care, Father, pride's the root o' all sin.

MOTILLA: And the root o' pride's riches.

PONTOCARRERO: You'll tear Spain t' pieces less you learn t' compromise—'tis the cornerstone o' good government.

MOTILLA: 'Tis the ignoble truce 'twixt duty and cowardice. Rather call 't by its proper name now, 'fraud'.

PONTOCARRERO: Call 't what you will, 'compromise', 'fraud', you hate 't cause you've no sense o' life's complexities.

MOTILLA: The ground has your knees, the world your conscience. Thanks t' you, plain dealing's dead.

PONTOCARRERO: Bend, accept less than you ask, less than you deserve. Bend, live and let live. Bend, or you'll break us.

MOTILLA: We're broken now. One fly hath corrupted the whole pot. You cared not f' justice, f' the poor, sick, lamed and blind. So Christ cared not f' us. Now he's made me the Divine instrument o' thy humiliation and fall. You stink like the sons o' Eli.

PONTOCARRERO: I'll not lose my temper, Father.

MOTILLA: Gi' thanks t' Him I let thee live t' repent o' thy vulgar furnishings, tawdry gowns, cheap geegaws ...

PONTOCARRERO: Vulgar?! Tawdry?! CHEAP?! I've the most exquisite taste in Europe, you crump-backed, crack-arsed Ethiopian!

The rich wall-drapes are pulled down to reveal grey panels covered with filth and graffiti.

MOTILLA: Curse on, 'tis sweeter music t' me than the sweet bells o' St Martin's.

PONTOCARRERO: I'll grind mustard wi' thy knees, sapscull!

MOTILLA: How shovel-mouth? I've stripped thee Jack-naked o' all power and influence. You've no weapons left. I canst stand here wi'out lifting my little finger and still crush thee flat and bloody. God's wi' me.

PONTOCARRERO: And I canst stand here eyeball t' bloodshot

eyeball wi'out speaking or twitching a belly muscle and yet ravage thy livered soul. God's wi' me.

MOTILLA: Prove 't!

PONTOCARRERO: T' the death!

They strip for action. PONTOCARRERO *takes off his gloves,* MOTILLA *slips the scapula and mantle off his shoulders. The room is now completely bare as they stand facing each other Down Stage Centre,* MOTILLA *in his white habit,* PONTOCARRERO *in black.*

MOTILLA: List, does hear? (*Pointing up.*) Wings. All around, hosts o' angels sweeping in out of the sun t' fight f' me. See 'em draw up bravely i' their battle lines, turning the sky white. The Angels o' Destruction hover there on my left flank, the Angels o' God's Wrath on my right, there. And see amid the smoky banners, the Seven Angels o' Punishment guard my centre—the fires, rods and plagues o' the Lord—Lahaliel, Makatiel, Shaftiel, Hatriel, Pusiel, Rozziel and Kushiel, the rigid one o' God.

PONTOCARRERO: The Angels o' Vengeance, Jehoel, Suriel, Zaggagel, Akatriel, Yefefiah, and Metatron the Chancellor o' Heaven command my centre. The Angels o' Thrones my right flank o'er there, and the Angels o' Principalities my left, see there, wi' silken streamers.

MOTILLA: The Angel o' Repentance, the Angel o' Prayer, the Angel o' Baptismal Waters, I ha' e'm all 'cept the Angel o' Mercy.

PONTOCARRERO: There's no place f' him on my side neither; Gabriel, get thee back wi' thy garland o' roses. My commander's Rafael, Regent o' the Sun, Prince o' the Presence, Healer o' Men, Archangel o' Wisdom, Sociability and Light. Angels, draw thy swords. Help me masticate the soul o' this man o' chaos.

MOTILLA: Michael, Angel o' the Final Reckoning, Weigher o' Souls, Conqueror o' Satan, help me destroy this sinner's lust-filled spirit as I destroyed his place and power.

PONTOCARRERO: The holy trumpets! Christ's virgin colours unfurl. Forward—f' Jesu and the Blessed Virgin!

MOTILLA: God's silver lances, pikes and hooks're raised. Forward—f' Jesu and the Blessed Saints!

PONTOCARRERO: C-h-a-r-g-e.

MOTILLA: C-h-a-r-g-e.

Their bodies go rigid. They make no movements whatsoever, except their eyes bulge as they focus all the power of their wills and hatred to crush each other.

Silence; then PONTOCARRERO *lets out a grunt of pain and* MOTILLA's *face contorts in agony. Neck muscles tighten, faces turn white with strain as they continue pounding each other in their imaginations.*

Suddenly blood pours from MOTILLA's *mouth and nose. It gushes down the front of his white habit, but he never takes his eyes off* PONTOCARRERO. *There is a sickening 'crack' as a bone snaps and* PONTOCARRERO's *arm is broken. It is quickly followed by another 'crack' as his right leg is smashed too. As he topples over the bloodstained* MOTILLA *shakes with silent, triumphant laughter.*

A fanfare sounds off and the doors Up Stage Centre are flung open by TWO ATTENDANTS, CARLOS *lurches in accompanied by* FROYLAN *and the* COURTIERS: ALBA, TORRES *and* MONTERREY.

As CARLOS *comes Down Stage* MOTILLA *bows respectfully but* PONTOCARRERO *remains helpless on the floor.* CARLOS *frowns.* FROYLAN *pulls* PONTOCARRERO *up painfully whilst the* OTHERS *gather solicitously around* MOTILLA. *With* FROYLAN's *help* PONTOCARRERO *finally stands unsteadily on his one good leg and bows.*

CARLOS: Whaaa . . .?

PONTOCARRERO: I believe I've broken my arm and leg, Your Majesty.

CARLOS: This's no time t' tell me o' thy aches and PAINS. We all have our problems. III've jus' spoken t' Mamaaaa.

MOTILLA: T' *Mamaaaa* . . .? I mean t' the Queen Mother? But the Queen Mother's dead, Sire; she lies still in Abraham's bosom.

CARLOS: NO sssshe lies STILL in mine. The dead're so much stronger, making lodging-houses o' our hearts. Not too late t' repay her love. Though I believe I die f' 't, I've signed the Will . . . (*Flourishes document.*) I make Mama's choice, José o' Bavaria heir t' the throne o' Spain! (*The* OTHERS *are stunned.*) Kings must CHOOSE. Mmmama waa me t' choose her friend, the Cardinal-Archbishop. WILT advise me, Your Eminence, as you advised my Mamaaaaa?

PONTOCARRERO: Yes, Sire. Always, Your Majesty.

The COURTIERS *standing Stage Left with* MOTILLA *quickly move over to* PONTOCARRERO *who leans heavily on* FROYLAN.

CARLOS: Mamaaa says I must choose a new Confessor. Your Eminence, help me choose. NOW.

PONTOCARRERO: May I suggest Father Froylan?

FROYLAN: The King's Confessor?! Me, Your Eminence? No, Sire, no, no, no. I'm not worthy o' the honour . . . (*Thoughtfully.*) But if I'm not, who is?

CARLOS: 'Tis settled, come Father Froylan. (*He turns to exit Stage Left.*)

MOTILLA: But Sire, what o' me? My godly dreams?

CARLOS (*turning back*): Mama says, GET THEE OUT FROM US.

He points at MOTILLA *and a great wind suddenly springs up.* CARLOS *and the* OTHERS *back away and exit Stage Right.* MOTILLA *tries to follow but the wind forces him back. In his desperate effort to follow them he rips off his bloodstained habit to reveal he is wearing underneath a hair-shirt, torn loincloth and wooden Cross round his neck.*

The wind increases in ferocity, blowing him backwards Stage Left. He raises the wooden Cross against it but is beaten back to his knees as the lights fade down to a Spot on him.

He is left kneeling, holding up the Cross and praying in the howling wind and darkness.

SCENE VI

The wind dies down as MOTILLA *prays.*

MOTILLA: And I was cast out o' Madrid into this wilderness, disgraced, hung up by the nostrils, half-dead half-alive, worse than either, 'cause neither. Arriving here i' Las Hurdes, abject in despair, I sought the Abbot Nilus and asked him how 't went i' this desert, this desolation? He poured water into a vessel and said: 'look on the water'. I looked but 'twas murky. After a little he said, 'look again, see how clear 'tis now'. I looked into the water and saw my face as i' a mirror. When I was in the world I couldst not see myself f' the turbulence, but now in this solitude I recognize all my defaults. I'm justly mortified, Lord. I'm fired and tested i' the furnace o' defeat. F' a priest must be forged o' the purest stuff if he's t' guide God's nation home. Now, according t' my strength I pray, fast, meditate and abide: a barnacle on eternity. I cast out lust long since but am still harried by pride. I'll learn t' forgive, yea e'en those who know *exactly* what they do, Lord. I'll bathe in the honey o' forgiveness, reach out t' Him quivering, longing f' the day when all longing, all desire, all seeking, seeing, hearing, hoping shall be God. Then He'll come by burning bush, pillar o' cloud saying 'rise up and follow me back and change the world in humbleness and loving kindness . . .' (*A* MES-SENGER *appears in front of him out of the darkness.*) Spiritus Sancti! Doest come out o' Zion wi' a message from the Blessed Saviour?

1ST MESSENGER: No, out o' Madrid wi' a message from the Blessed Cardinal-Archbishop o' Toledo. He says, 'live and let live'.

MOTILLA: Oh the wingy mysteries o' Christ's mercy! T'know all is t' forgive all, I forgive all, I forgive all, live and let live *arrx* . . .

MOTILLA *gives a tiny gasp as the* MESSENGER *coolly slits his throat. Looking up at the* MESSENGER *in disbelief, he slowly falls, gurgling hoarsely. The* MESSENGER *calmly wipes his knife on the dying man's hair-shirt.*

1ST MESSENGER: Though he be condemned f' 't in the next world, a man's gotta make a living in this. I'll seek absolution after I've got me a fortune. And wi' sins like mine it's going t' *take* a fortune t' absolve 'em. I'll devote a third portion o' 't to the Society o' Jesus. That shouldst see me safe in Paradise. You need money t' enter God's house . . . (MOTILLA *claws the air.*) Only the poor can die easy. F' 'tis small grief t' leave hunger and cold, but t' forsake full barns, full purses, soft beds and beauteous women and go t' death's empty kingdom, this is terror. Wi' a job like mine, you gets t' be a bit o' a philosopher. (MOTILLA *makes the sign of the Cross, gives a final gasp and rolls backwards, dead.*) Glad he were the forgiving type. Some o' 'em get very bitter. (*Looks at* MOTILLA *again.*) A neat job. No mess. The work o' a pro, no question.

Though the Spot stays on the dead body, another Spot follows the 1ST MESSENGER *as he walks Up Stage Right. He meets a* 2ND MESSENGER.

2ND MESSENGER: Message from the Cardinal-Archbishop— 'live and let live'.

1ST MESSENGER: 'Tis done.

The 2ND MESSENGER *nods and stabs the* 1ST MESSENGER *brutally in the stomach. He staggers back as the other repeatedly knives him.*

1ST MESSENGER (*scornfully*): Amateur!

He falls back dead. The 2ND MESSENGER *wipes his knife and hands on the dead man and walks diagonally Up Stage Right in a Spot. The Spot on* MOTILLA *fades out as the* 2ND MESSENGER *meets a* 3RD.

3RD MESSENGER: From the Cardinal-Archbishop—'live and let live'.

2ND MESSENGER: *Ahhhhhhhh.*

The 2ND MESSENGER *screams in terror but is cut down before he can escape. The* 3RD MESSENGER *repeats the actions of his predecessors and walks off Up Stage Right in a Spot whistling. The Spot on the* 1ST MESSENGER *fades out as we hear a voice off Up Stage Right.*

4TH MESSENGER (*off*): From the Cardinal-Archbishop—'live and let live'.

3RD MESSENGER (*off*): *Ahhhhhhhh.*

The scream is followed by a thud as the body hits the ground, then whistling. The Spot on the 2ND MESSENGER *fades out and we hear diminishing snatches of conversation as the cycle of assassination continues in the darkness.*

5TH MESSENGER (*off*): . . . Cardinal . . . live and let . . .

4TH MESSENGER (*off*): *Ahhhhhhhh.*

The inevitable scream dies away.

SCENE VII

Birdsong. Dawn lights up on woodland clearing. Morning mist and an impression of surrounding trees. TORRES *and* ALMIRANTE *with a flat, leather case wait Stage Right stamping to keep warm whilst* ALBA *wanders about.*

ALMIRANTE: Our Cardinal-Archbishop's happy. Father Motilla conveniently dead and his assassins stretched in a bloody line from Las Hurdes t' the sea. I'm t' be relieved o' command o' the new army, whilst he negotiates peace wi' the French. *Peace.* That cassocked traitor's sunk so low not even Christ's tears could raise him t' the depths o' degradation. He'll leave us wi'out heir or honour.

TORRES: The Cid no longer rides out. Honour's fled into the pages o' my books. I've shelves filled wi' honour.

ALBA: There was honour here once, my lords. This used t' be

the favourite duelling ground f' the best bloods o' Madrid, in my youth. I pierced three gallants m'self on this very spot in one afternoon. Challenged the first f' looking at me sideways, the second f' staring straight at me, the third f' not looking at me at all! Matter o' honour. Had t' fight, don't y' see. But you don't, my lord Almirante. A true grandee can only accept the challenge o' equals. Master Tom-o-my-Thumb's not o' thy rank or blood.

ALMIRANTE: I chose t' ignore the differences, as I ignored the insult when the Queen was high in favour. But now she's down, out and vulnerable, I must protect her reputation close. 'Stead o' great glory I'll make do wi' a little vengeance. I feel in a killing mood. (*Takes off cloak.*) Our midget Zany must be taught a lasting lesson.

RAFAEL *enters Stage Left with his father* MORRA. *He, too, carries a flat case, and is suffering from a hangover. The two dwarfs bow formally and cross to* ALBA *Stage Centre.* ALMIRANTE *and* TORRES *do the same.*

MORRA: My lords, I act as second f' my son Rafael de Morra in this matter.

TORRES: And I act as second f' my lord, Almirante de la Castilla.

ALBA: 'Tis my Catholic duty t' attempt a reconciliation 'twixt opposing parties. Will the challenger make an apology?

ALMIRANTE: A small apology'd suffice.

MORRA: My son isn't here t' make apologies, string beads, or juggle soot, but t' fight!

ALBA: The party challenged has the right t' choose weapons.

TORRES: My principal's chosen pistols at eight paces 'stead o' swords, not wishing t' place himself at an unfair advantage due t' the unusual circumstances.

MORRA: Unusual circumstances? What unusual circumstances? I recognize no unusual circumstances. A de Morra accepts no favours. My son'll fight on foot or horseback, wi' a sword, pike, halberd, dagger, mace or cudgel—rocks if need be.

RAFAEL: Father, weapons've been named. We fight wi' pistols

at eight paces, though I'd be happier wi' puff pastry at eighty.

ALMIRANTE *and* RAFAEL *open their cases and take out their pistols.*

ALBA: At my signal walk eight paces, turn and fire at pleasure. A misfire's t' be reckoned a shot and a snap or non-cock a misfire.

ALBA, *with* TORRES *and* MORRA *on either side of him, steps back Up Stage.* RAFAEL *and* ALMIRANTE *stand back to back despite the ridiculous difference in their heights. At a signal from* ALBA *they start to walk away,* RAFAEL *having to hold his heavy pistol in both hands and his tiny steps making the distance between them ludicrously small.*

ALBA: One, two, three, four, five, six, seven, eight.

They stop. ALMIRANTE *turns first and quickly fires—a stream of water over* RAFAEL*: his weapon is a water-pistol. As* RAFAEL *is drenched* ALMIRANTE *roars with laughter and* TORRES *and* ALBA, *seeing what has happened, join in.* MORRA *is white-faced with rage.*

As the laughter continues a shot rings out: RAFAEL *has fired. The laughter stops instantly.* ALMIRANTE *spins slowly round, drops his weapon and puts his hand to his forehead; it is covered with blood. As he sinks to his knees,* TWO CIRCUS CLOWNS *in huge shoes, baggy pants, red noses and yellow wigs rush on Stage Left amid drum-rolls, honks and whistles and stuff a red rag in* ALMIRANTE's *mouth and drag him off dead, Stage Right.*

Lights out as coloured balloons float down from the Flies.

SCENE VIII

Canons thunder a salute out of the darkness. Lights up on the Royal Reception Room and the whole Court plus the French Ambassador, REBENAC. *Amid triumphant fanfares the Court advances ceremonially Down Stage and lines up, waving regally to the audience.*

PONTOCARRERO: We gi' thanks t' God. Spain is at peace; f' by His great mercy a treaty's been signed wi' the French, English and Dutch William at Ryswick in this year o' Our Lord, 1697, whereby His Majesty Louis XIV o' France doth gi' back all territories conquered; Luxembourg, Mons, Ath, Coustrai and Catalonia, including the towns o' Gerona, Rosas and Barcelona. Spain's Empire remains intact, her glory undimmed.

With one arm hanging stiffly by his side PONTOCARRERO *hands the treaty to* CARLOS *who holds it up. Wild cheering and more fanfares as the Court move formally back Up Stage into the Reception Room where the coloured balloons are still on the floor.*

DR BRAVO: Where're your Mars's, malefics and mumbos now, Master Gongora? You prognosticated darkness f' Spain and death f' me. But see, Spain's at peace and I'm alive. Eyes badger-bright, heart and spleen in working order. Feel this bone and muscle (*Jabs him in the stomach*), smell that sweet breath. (*Breathes in his face.*) Admit 't, sir, you're wrong again.

GONGORA: I don't understand what's wrong, but I'm not wrong. You're wrong, the world's wrong, but I'm not wrong. I've charted and re-charted the star-courses. By all the signs you're dead. First my teeth, now this. I suspect foul play. You're dead but won't lie down.

DR BRAVO *laughs but* FROYLAN, *who has been listening to them, nods thoughtfully.*

The Court is now assembled in the Reception Room. The men bow deeply and the women curtsey to CARLOS.

CARLOS: Aaaa let our Brother Louis Beelezebub—er, Louis the Blessed—know how greatly weeee love him.

REBENAC: Happily, Sire. And may I hope this new found spirit o' diplomacy grows twixt our nations.

PONTOCARRERO: 'Twill. I've sacrificed too much f' peace .. (*There is a distant shout of 'Live and let live', a cry and a thud.*) Didst hear 't?

They look blank. CARLOS *gestures and all the* COURTIERS *rise.*
DR BRAVO *hurries to him.*

DR BRAVO: Sire, you need rest. Thou hast been waving on that balcony f' a full five minutes.

CARLOS: 'Tis nothing. We royals 're born wi' rubber wrists. Happy day. WWWhy art not looking haaa happy, Maaaadam?

ANA: Joey's dead. Father Motilla's dead. The Almirante de Castilla's dead.

CARLOS: You shouldst still beee happy, 'tis merely PERSONAL. If they're strong they doooon't DDDie. Maaamaaa didn't die. She chose my Cardinal-Archbishop and now all we lost's been restored, Mama knows . . .

ANA: Art blind? Louis only gi's back what he conquered t' make himself so popular his grandson Phillip'll be made heir t' the Spanish throne wi'out him firing another shot or losing another Frog's leg.

CARLOS: Madam, I haaa jus' chosen my heir—José o' Bavaria.

Applause from the COURTIERS *and sycophantic congratulations.*
Furious, ANA *absently plucks the feathers from the dead* PARROT
on her arm.

REBENAC: But Sire, you casn't choose José.

CARLOS: I c–c–c–c–c–a . . .?!

REBENAC: Sire, José's dead.

CARLOS: *Whaaaa . . .*

REBENAC: Tertian fever.

GONGORA: Ah, my beautiful malefics! Betrayals, conspiracies and deaths! I was right.

REBENAC: He died three days since. I don't understand, is Spanish Intelligence so slow?

ANA: Slow? Why d'you think there're no wooden statues carved o' Spaniards? They can't find pieces o' wood thick enough.

PONTOCARRERO: 'Tis the roads.

CARLOS: Dead? Dead? Whaa . . . words pass through me . . .

ANA: Mama knows best! Why didn't she know José was dead? Happen her beady eyes were blinded by hell-fire, pit-fire? Nothing changes. You still ha' t' choose Carlos: Philip Bourbon or Charles o' Austria.

CARLOS: *Eeeeh. Eeeeh. Eeeeh.*

PONTOCARRERO: 'T does change. Now God has blessed Spain wi' an honourable peace, He'll bless thy penis-member, Sire, if you flash 't at him.

CARLOS: *I tried . . . tried . . . tried . . . tried . . .*

He careers round, screeching and stamping on the coloured balloons, exploding them in his fury. He finally collapses on the floor beside one last black balloon. PONTOCARRERO *bends over him.*

PONTOCARRERO: You can produce an heir, Sire. The Virgin Mother'll help you.

FROYLAN: She won't. And he can't.

All look round in astonishment.

CARLOS (*clawing the balloon*): Heaaa my Confessor assails me wi' pure truth . . . 'tis my wife, my wife's SINSSSS . . . HER fault.

FROYLAN: No, Sire, 'tis you. You're impotent, Sire: coeundi, erigendi, generandi, *Impotentia.*

Stunned silence. The balloon bursts in CARLOS's *hands. He staggers up.*

CARLOS: IMPO didst you say IMPO . . .? *Eeeeh*, my body's turned t' glass, IIII'm breaking. Eminence, yyyy chose José o' Bavaria f' me and THIS impotenting priest . . .!

PONTOCARRERO (*low*): Father, you'll destroy us. Remember you're a Jesuit. Equivocate. *Be devious.*

FROYLAN: I'm the King's Confessor. In matters concerning the Society o' Jesus I humbly obey, but in those pertaining t' the confessional I submit only t' the true will o' God. Sire, I seek audience—alone.

ANA: After such an insult you'd best seek mercy.

CARLOS: IMPO . . . my belly's glass, they canst see my heart and bowels . . . Withdraw.

PONTOCARRERO *is about to protest but* CARLOS *waves him*

away with a tiny frightened gesture. All exit backwards Stage Left and Right. Only FROYLAN *remains.*

FROYLAN: Doest achieve full erection, Sire?

CARLOS: Cu ca po fo bigger than an elephant's trunk, stiffer than a stake, hhhhhheavier than bell-clapper, *b-o-n-g* . . .

FROYLAN: Chapter VI o' the 'Malleus Maleficarium' states: 'If a man's virile member's erect but he casn't penetrate, and the seminal ducts're blocked so the vital juices're dammed back or fruitlessly spilled, then that man's impotent by reason o' *witchcraft*.'

CARLOS: WWWWW . . .?

FROYLAN: Thy impotence isn't physical, but magical. The fault's not in thee, Sire.

CARLOS: Not mmmm fault . . .?

FROYLAN: You're bewitched, Sire . . . (*He produces a book.*) Zacharias Vicecomes writes i' the 'Complementum Artis Exorcisticae' on the signs o' bewitchment: (*He reads.*) 'A man's truly bewitched if he's vexed by solid foods and molested by much vomiting; (CARLOS *retches*) if he feeleth a daily gnawing i' his belly; (CARLOS *rubs his stomach*) if he hath an ache i' his kidneys, throbbing i' his neck, splinters i' his head, nails i' his heart and excretes bucketsfull o' worms hourly . . .'

CARLOS (*slowly*): 'S me . . . 's me . . . 's me . . .

He takes the book and reads with difficulty as the room is suffused with dark red light.

FROYLAN: 'Tis magic that frustrates us, not brute reality. Bewitchment's the cause o' all our present ills; 't holds us in a dream. Witches and magicians run rampant. E'ery night pentacles're drawn, odours o' sulphur rise, black candles lit, crucifixes defiled, blood drunk, Satan's grey arse kissed: 'O Emperor Lucifer, Master o' all rebellious Spirits, I beg . . . Aglon, Tetragram, Vaycheon, Stimulamthon.'—Thus Satan's Pit-legions're summoned; his grand almoner Dagon; his banker Asmoden; his Master o' Ceremonies Verdelet. Jean Wiere, physician t' Duque de Cleres, calculated Satan had

7,409,127 devils commanded by 76 Infernal Princes. 7,409,127.
Idiot! Idiot! I've proved there're exactly 175,806,417 devils.
175,806,417. No more, no less. That's 2 and 1/6 o' a devil per
person . . . (CARLOS *trembles*.) Ne'er fear, Sire, cometh the
hour, cometh the man. I'm ready armed in the sweet name o'
Jesus Christ Our Lord. But first, Sire, we must confirm thou
art bewitched and then uncover the foul agent o' Satan
responsible. 'Tis certain, as always, God'll maintain his
habitual silence, so I'll command the one being who knows
the truth t' tell us—Lucifer, the Evil One. *Command*, not ask.
F' 'tis heresy t' ask a favour o' the Devil.

CARLOS (*looking round*): Where doest find him?

FROYLAN: In the bodies o' the possessed. At this moment I'm
exorcising a fiend-sick nest o' nuns from the Cangas Convent
who're most truly possessed. I say truly, f' 't has become
fashionable o' late to simulate possession. But they casn't
fool me, I smell the dying flowers, see the scorpion-demons
peering out o' bloodshot eyeballs, *there, there*. Satan spoke t'
me from the left nostril o' a nun last month, telling me I'd rise
t' high office. He's still there, i' the intestines o' that poor Bride
o' Christ. I could but weaken him then, now I'll drag him
forth and command him in the name o' the Lord God, t'
speak the truth concerning your mighty penis-member.

CARLOS: Quick-quick-quick.

FROYLAN: The Inspector General must be informed, though he's
more interested in heresy than witchcraft. Blind! Blind! We
go forth, Sire, t' combat Lucifer, wi' faith as our perfect shield.
(CARLOS'*s legs buckle*.) Evil only takes hold through weakness.
It enters one o' six openings: eyes, ears, mouth, nose, navel,
penis, vagina and feeds on our hate, becoming a swelling wart
on the soul, drawing strength from our every selfish thought
and act. All impulses o' tenderness're blocked, love casn't pass
through us f' we solidify. And then wickedness takes on its
own reality, spawning out little limpet-demons made i' the
image o' our sins: gluttons 've pig-demons, misers sucker-

demons, murderers tarantula-demons. We must be ready, Sire. (*He produces a three-pronged fork inscribed with symbols.*) 'Tis a Paracelsian Trident, a blessed and magnetized blasting rod o' demons. These three prongs act as lightning arresters, discharging accumulated magnetism. Skewered demons burn on the tips. (*He stabs the air with the trident, then hands it to* CARLOS.) Remember, Hell's hordes mayn't be visible, but they'll be there, ready t' pounce when we fight the Devil raging i' the Nuns o' Cangas.

CARLOS (*stabbing the air*): The Nuns o' Cangas!

A faint sound of female voices off Stage Right, singing the hymn, 'Quem terra pontus aethera . . .'

FROYLAN: Evil ne'er fades. Every sin since the first Adam breathes in us. Every depravity since the first Cain chokes our trussed lungs. The Nuns o' Cangas're drowning, grown hideous i' their pain, terror, as ne'er before, horror as ne'er before . . .

CARLOS (*stabbing wildly*): The Nuns o' Cangas! The Nuns o' Cangas!

As the music and singing grows louder a stained glass mediaeval fresco of St Michael slaying a Dragon is lowered Up Stage Centre.

The lights grow brighter, whilst CARLOS *compulsively stabs the air and* FROYLAN *turns Stage Right to face the Nuns of Cangas.*

SCENE IX

Three gentle, middle-aged NUNS: *the demure* SISTER INEZ, *the voluptuous* SISTER RENATA *and the beautiful* SISTER JUANA, *enter solemnly.* SISTER JUANA *carries a large Cross with meat hooks hanging from the arms.*

NUNS (*singing*): '. . . Beata caeli nuntio/fecunda sancto Spiritu,/ desideratus gentibus/cujus per alvum fuses est. Gloria Tibi Domine/qui natus es de virgine/cum Patre et sancto Spiritu/ in sempiterna saecula.'

FROYLAN (*putting on large, dark-lensed spectacles*): I'd go blind wi'out these protective eye-barnacles. Mark, Sire, the haloes o' inextinguishable guilt about their heads. In nomine Patris et Filii et Spiritus Sancti.

The NUNS *have stopped humbly in front of* FROYLAN *and a trembling* CARLOS. FROYLAN *makes the sign of the Cross over them and takes out a small phial of holy water.*

FROYLAN: Foul spirit, in the name o' our Lord Jesus Christ, be rooted out and be put t' flight from this creature o' God.

He flings some holy water into SISTER INEZ'*s face.*

SISTER INEZ: Fans opened next t' me, hundreds in my time. Dancing, spinspread, 'cross a Continent, a moment later, Naples. Years o' light-music, ah those spreads, those bright distances. But my family drew a curtain in front o' my face t' save a dowry, one more Saint on the calendar: Asia never returned. I had *their* wills in *my* head. Infinity won me, untouched by human hands. Now trees wi' old branches. Now my mornings touch my evenings, loneliness wi'out solitude, solitude wi'out being alone. Forty years' waste, brain waste, heart waste, wall t' wall waste, seven hundred thousand nothings since Monday *ahhh!*

She cries out in fright as FROYLAN *who has been circling her suddenly seizes his opportunity and throws his stole round her neck.* SISTERS RENATA *and* JUANA *remain quite still by the Cross.*

FROYLAN (*to* CARLOS): The little demons! See, see they begin t' jump off her. Keep thy mouth shut, Sire, else they'll hop 'twixt thy yellowing molars. Strike, Sire! Strike! (*Whilst* CARLOS *frantically stabs the air* FROYLAN *pulls the struggling* INEZ *close and makes the sign of the Cross on her forehead.*) Satan, enemy o' man, cause o' all chaos, the Word made flesh commands thee, Jesus o' Nazareth commands thee, come out from her!

SISTER INEZ: If the light in me's darkness, how dark's the darkness? Chaos's my true Lord! Blind chance rules the world!

She breaks free and stands by the Cross, whilst SISTER RENATA

B—5

curtsies and takes her place in front of FROYLAN *who throws holy water in her face as* CARLOS *continues to stab the air.*

SISTER RENATA: The beast's missing. I lost his face in the mosses and the shadows. After so much frontal punching, fiery tit-tarting, my nest's cold. Oh Paolo, Paolo, you undid my neck-string, lifted my gown and came like dew falling from the grass; sunshaft 'tween my thighs. Then dice-throwing death took him dead on the wrong side, dimlap on the shore. Widowed and walled in a day and I'm ill every time I wake, all the day ill. Thy tongue isn't f' eating and speaking but f' jousting, moistening, tipping the velvet and stirring mayonnaise! I'm a Bride o' Christ, why doesn't Jesus come do 't f' me?! Quick, quick, 'afore decay thrusts its blade and bellies blotch and buttocks go slack and the young wheat trembles, *ahhh!*

She cries out as FROYLAN *finally pounces and throws the stole round her neck. She struggles but he jerks her close and makes the sign of the Cross on her forehead.*

FROYLAN: Satan, enemy o' man, cause o' all chaos, the Word made flesh commands thee, Jesus o' Nazareth commands thee—come out from her!

SISTER RENATA: I defy the crucifix, deny the sacrifice. Chaos's my true Lord! Blind chance rules the world!

She breaks free and goes to the Cross, whilst SISTER JUANA *curtsies and silently takes her place in front of* FROYLAN *who throws holy water at her. She tries to speak but can make only gasping noises.*

FROYLAN: Satan's proving eel-slippery, Sire. 'Tis our last chance t' hook him. (*He suddenly throws the stole round* SISTER JUANA's *neck, she struggles but he pulls her close and makes the sign of the Cross on her forehead.*) I adjure thee ancient serpent, by the judge o' the Quick and the Dead, by thy Maker, and the Maker o' the world—come out from her! (SISTER JUANA *breaks free.*) Yield and answer! Yield and answer! YIELD AND ANSWER!

SISTER JUANA *speaks in a deep voice.*

SISTER JUANA: Hello out there? Somebody call? I heard voices. The Universe's already 98 per cent dead but I've still a thousand million years o' living t' do before the sun finally turns cold, black and dwarfish and it's all bets off.

FROYLAN: Art Satan?

SISTER JUANA: The very same; the first mover o' the world. The name's 'daemon' which means, 'knowledge'. Would you like to know how Helen looked and what blind Homer sang? How parallels t' infinity meet and unseen stars leave their frozen traces in the sky? Why some men die and others 'scape the plague? Let me tempt you, laddie. The Universe lies open. Just ask.

FROYLAN:Has His Majesty's penis-member magically withered? Is he bewitched?

SISTER JUANA: Ah the pitiless banality, the remorseless drip o' human stupidity. Yes, he's bewitched.

FROYLAN: Praise be t' God! I knew 't. You're bewitched, Sire!

CARLOS (*joyfully, waving trident*): BBBBB eeee I'm bewitched ... 's not my fault, 's nothing wrong. IIIII'm jus' bewitched bewitched, bewitched...! (*Stops: slowly.*) *I'm b-e-w-i-t-c-h-e-d!*

FROYLAN: Satan I command thee, who hath bewitched His Majesty?

SISTER JUANA: You don't really want t' know. You'd miss the joys o' finding out f' yourselves. One clue: they want the French fleur-de-lys t' come t' Spain. Now go, search and destroy!

FROYLAN: Satan, I command thee: who bewitched His Majesty? Who? Who?

CARLOS: Wwwhhhoooo?!

FROYLAN: *In God's name, name names!*

The light begins to fade as the NUNS *stop eating and chant gently.*

NUNS: Duque de Alba, Pedro Alvarez, Victor Amadeus, Inez Ayala, Mendiza de Balthazar, Dr Gasper Bravo, Don Sebastien

de Coles, Father Don Froylan, Francisco Garrigo, Marquis
Gudames, Queen Ana de Neuburg, Queen Mariana de
Austria, Conde Medellion, (*frightened whispers in the darkness
now form a background to the endless roll-call*) Duque de Monter-
rey, Duque de Medina de la Torres, Father Don Motilla,
José de Olmo, Conte de Oropesa, Cardinal Archbishop
Pontocarrero, Francisco Ramos, Juan Tomas Rocaberti, Don
Francisco Ponquillo, Condesa de la Vanquyon . . .

    *The roll-call fades away, leaving the frightened murmurs in the
darkness growing louder.*

SCENE X

Lights up on the Throne Room where the COURTIERS *whisper and
wait nervously. They include* LADIES-IN-WAITING, ALBA,
MONTERREY, TORRES, GONGORA, DR BRAVO, BELEPSCH,
and the Dancing Master ANTONIO. RAFAEL *sits on the edge of the
throne platform drinking. Down Stage Left* ANA *talks to* PONTO-
CARRERO *whilst stroking the moulting carcass of the* PARROT *on
her arm.*

ANA: No one's safe from your King's Confessor.
PONTOCARRERO: I've spawned an incubus. In all other particu-
    lars he's clerk-humble but feels divinely empowered t' save
    Spain from rampant sorcery. The prospect's midnight black
    f' us all, (*shudders*) he's *sincere*.
ANA: He seeks out witches as eager as a pig snouting truffles.
PONTOCARRERO: 'Tis a bad time t' be plagued by such lethal
    loons. Spain's turned rebellious in her hunger and despair.
    Madrid's a vast abscess. At this moment His Majesty's in
    greater danger from his own subjects than Satan's. And he still
    has to choose an heir now José o' Bavaria's dead. Philip
    Bourbon's unthinkable so I propose t' forward your claimant,
    Your Majesty, the Archduke Charles.

ANA: You adjust easily, Your Eminence. But first break your Jesuit Judas.

PONTOCARRERO: The Church proclaims witches exist and the King that he's bewitched. Whoever opposes Father Froylan flouts Church and State.

ANA (*angrily plucking the last feather out of the* PARROT): It sticks! The Queen o' Spain trembling afore a stiff-rumped cleric whose mother took in boarders.

BELEPSCH: Now at least Your Majesty, you've someone t' hate again.

ANA: He's not big enough; (*softly*) eeehh there's no one left big enough f' me t' hate.

She throws aside the dead PARROT, *now completely denuded of feathers, as* CARLOS *enters silently Stage Left leaning on* FATHER FROYLAN's *shoulder and followed by* TWO MONKS.

The men bow low, the women curtsey. ANA *falls in behind* CARLOS *and* FROYLAN *as they cross to the throne, with the priest continually whispering in the King's ear and gesturing furtively to the bowed* COURTIERS. CARLOS *nods and slumps on the throne.*

ANA *watches in fury as* FROYLAN *whispers again and* CARLOS *mutters incoherently. The* COURTIERS *rise and the King gestures to* FROYLAN.

FROYLAN: My lords, Satan swore by our Saviour's blood, that his earthly agent suppressed His Majesty's virile member, blocked 'ts love juices. The bewitched organ's been fumigated wi' incense and doused in a thimble o' holy water. But the only lasting cure's the destruction o' the Devil's agent. Lucifer refused t' name him, though he named a thousand names. F' witches're not only those who cast black spells but whoso'er does anything which casn't be explained by nature or art. E'en now, suspects're questioned close, wi' rack, boot and Wheel i' the dungeons o' the Inquisition. Their devil-marks—warts, moles and pimples're being pierced and tested wi' red hot needles. (*A* LADY-IN-WAITING *faints.*) At His Majesty's request 't falls on me t' gather in all suspects f' questioning and testing. You my lords must help. F' under command, Lucifer revealed his agent's secret love o' France and I believe he or she resides here at Court. (*All eye each other suspiciously.*) E'en now you mayst be standing next t' the agent o' Satan. (*All shift warily.*) Happen there's more than one. Look f' the signs, my lords. Witches casn't weep . . . (ANTONIO *starts crying*), feel pain . . . (TORRES *pinches himself and cries out*), but do wear talismen. (MONTERREY *tears off his jewel pendant.*) Report any who act strange, have sudden success—that's a most damaging sign, success. T' save His Majesty I've summoned the newly appointed Royal Witch-Catcher. The Witch-Catcher's famous instrument can detect suspect sorcery at ten paces, night or day. There's no protection in blood, rank, wealth or piety. So let the guilty sweat. List, list the Witch-Catcher cometh . . .

There is an eerie sucking sound Off Stage Left. The COURTIERS *turn fearfully towards it. It grows louder and finally* THERESA DIEGO, *the Head Washerwoman, enters dressed in a gaudy pink farthingale, vulgar jewels and a small fur muff clamped delicately over her nose.*

RAFAEL: Why, 'tis Old Mother Bagwash!

The titter is immediately silenced as THERESA *sweeps Up Stage and curtsies clumsily before* CARLOS, *who waves his hand impatiently.* THERESA *rises as* FROYLAN *comes down to her.*

FROYLAN: Mistress Diego'll pass amongst you, sniffing out the Devil's own.

THERESA: Thank you, Father. (*She carefully removes her nose muff.*) Ha' no fear, Your Majesty, though this room's heavy wi' the odour o' thy divinity, I'll smell out soiled souls as surely as soiled clothes. All stink different: murderers o' grey hemp, plague-carriers o' sour apples, lepers o' dead mice. Witches've the heaviest kind o' crotch smell. They casn't hide 't though they bathe in camphor and sweet aloes. 'Tis too skung-strong t' wash away. (*She dabs her nose with a large, lace handkerchief.*) Wi' your permission, Sire, I'll nose a stink.

CARLOS *gurgles impatiently;* RAFAEL *lifts his flask in a toast.*

RAFAEL: T' the grindstone!

Ignoring him, THERESA *slowly walks between the apprehensive* COURTIERS *sniffing the air, followed by* FROYLAN *and the* TWO MONKS.

Slowly passing PONTOCARRERO *and* TORRES *she steps in front of* GONGORA. *He trembles as her sniffing grows louder.*

GONGORA: 'Sn't me! 'Sn't me! *Him, 'tis him.* (*He points hysterically at* DR BRAVO.) Bravo's been dead two weeks, I calculated it t' the last ascendant cusp and malicious square. He's carrying his corpse, his body's hollow. 'Tis *necromancy.* He's made a pact with the Devil t' survive his own death!

DR BRAVO: You half-dead, toothless gusset, my breath disturbs the air. My lord Torres, was I dead when I cured thee o' the piles, or you, my lord, o' the hernia? *Ha-ha . . .* (*No one laughs.*) I know the difference 'twixt life and death, 'tis my profession. See, I talk, move, jerk my head, roll my eyes in wonder. (*Holds out hands.*) My hand trembles . . . that's life . . . see . . . ?

He falters as THERESA *sniffs loudly in front of him.*

THERESA: Fe, fi, fo. I smell odour mortis. And the Satan's fungy stench. *This man's suspect.*

FROYLAN: Yes, who had better chance t' damage His Majesty's royal penis-member under the guise o' healing 't.

TORRES: Roman physicians always poisoned their emperors. 'Quis custodiet ipsos Custodes?' Juvenal asked in the Sixth Satire—or was 't the Fifth?

GONGORA: He's now a deadly dead man, Satan's man, not my best friend Bravo who pulled out my best teeth.

CARLOS: *Taaaaaeeeeeeekk.*

The TWO HOODED MONKS *take* DR BRAVO *by the arm and escort him out.*

DR BRAVO: Sire, Sire, I've keep thee alive, keep me alive now. My lords, help me—laced louse-traps! You'll cry out f' Dr Bravo, when you've your distempers again, your hard pad, foot-rot, gas gangrene, anthrax, red worms, oak poisoning, liver fluke and *swine-fever* . . .

Even as the MONKS *drag him off Stage Left* THERESA *continues her menacing prowl. She stops and snorts in front of* ANTONIO *who jumps back in fright.*

ANTONIO: 'Tis my perfume, Mistress Diego. Body aromatics— distilled water o' jilly-flowers t' keep skin clear and bright. (THERESA *sniffs again.*) Essence o' lavender, citron peel and oil o' spike, t' take off spots and wrinkles. Innocent aromatics. Mistress, innocent aromatics—red pomatum f' plump lips, white paste f' hard hands and . . .

THERESA: Not all the rose-water i' Shiraz can hide the fungy smell rising from thy soul. *This man's suspect.*

FROYLAN: Yes . . . the fleur de lys! Didst not the Devil confess his witch was o' the French Party.

ALBA: Yes, I always suspected Monsieur Antonio o' treachery wi' his French words, perfumes, dances, laces, windows, letters . . .

CARLOS: *Taaaaaaeeeeeekk.*

The MONKS *take* ANTONIO *by the arms.*

ANTONIO: I'll put away my French words! Mon Dieu! The Court'll be wi'out a Dancing Master if I'm taken, Sire, 'saut, saut, petit saut'. No one's e'er called me a witch, Sire, bitch yes, but not witch!

He is dragged off Stage Right.

ANA: 'Tis true. Witch or bitch, 'twill leave us wi'out a Dancing Master, we'll be the laughing stock o' every Court i' Europe 'cause o' this drab's nose.

But CARLOS *excitedly waves her aside and nods repeatedly to* THERESA. *As she resumes her prowling,* RAFAEL *staggers up and follows her around, parodying her movements, honking and sniffing his own armpits and the soles of his shoes. The* COURTIERS *are too terrified to laugh.*

Ignoring him THERESA *stops in front of* BELEPSCH *who screws up her face in distaste.*

BELEPSCH: Ma'am, tell this gravy-eyed peasant t' stand back from me. She stinks o' lower parts.

THERESA: 'Tis honest stink, not devil's stink; the stink o' my soiled world where I've seen the rot beneath the ribbon and lace. The washhouse'll be working late tonight. Bowels rumble, noble arses open wide. I canst smell fear. I've made diarrhetics o' y' all! (*She sniffs triumphantly.*) Sniff . . . Sniff . . . Sniff . . . (*The* COURTIERS *join in sniffing loudly: she suddenly turns on* BELEPSCH.) *This woman's suspect.*

MONTERREY: Yes, she's greedy f' gold. All witches're greedy f' gold!

BELEPSCH: Helfen Sie mir Ihre Majestät.

ANA: Carlos, the Countess Belepsch's my dearest companion. I'll not've her taken.

FROYLAN: If she be innocent then the Holy Inquisition'll soon discover 't and no harm done, 'cept a gouged eyeball or two. Happen the Queen's other reasons f' protecting this German suspect?

PONTOCARRERO: Jus' reasons o' the heart, Father. This's not the place f' such sentiments, Ma'am, later, later.

CARLOS: *Taaaaaeeeeeekk.*

The MONKS *escort the frantic* BELEPSCH *out.*

BELEPSCH: Save me, Your Majesty . . .! Remember the picnics on the Rhine . . . the Spanish gold we've confiscated together . . . I'm no witch . . .! (*Singing hysterically.*) 'Schlaf, Kinderl, schlaf./Der Tod sitzt auf der Stang/Er hat ein weissen Kittel an/ er will die bösen Kinder han/Schlaf, Kinderl, Schlaf . . !'

Even as she exits Stage Left between the MONKS, THERESA *resumes her search and the terrified* COURTIERS *join in sniffing each other.*

Delighted, RAFAEL *capers up to* FROYLAN, *sniffs him and cowers back in disgust at the smell, then scampers after* THERESA *mimicking her exaggeratedly 'genteel' manners. Suddenly she points at him.*

THERESA: *This buffoon's suspect.*

RAFAEL: Is 't true your husband left you the day he recovered his eyesight? *honk, honk.*

THERESA: I smell Satan. *This buffoon's suspect.*

All eyes turn to CARLOS *who looks uncertainly at the laughing dwarf.*

FROYLAN: Sire, laughter's a true mark o' Lucifer: the damnable element, pip o' the first apple. We follow Satan when we laugh.

ANA: I delivered up my close favourite t' save thy precious stump, Carlos. If she's suspect, so 's this laughing Tom. He killed the Almirante de Castilla!

CARLOS: *Taaaaeeeeeekk.*

The HOODED MONKS *cross to* RAFAEL *who stops laughing and stares at* CARLOS *in astonishment.*

RAFAEL: I'll break my bladder-stick, bury 't deep and drown Mother Bunch's jokes e'en deeper. My pole-star's gone a-wandering. My lords be merry and only promise on your oath, you'll come dance on my grave.

TORRES: Where'll you be buried?

RAFAEL: At sea. You ha' the wrong man. I'm Josephus Rex. Poor Jo-King, *honk, honk.* Keep sniffing, my lords and ladies. Sniff! Sniff! Sniff . . . !

The COURTIERS *resume their desperate sniffing and sing as the lights fade down and* RAFAEL *exits between the* TWO MONKS *Stage Right.*

ALL (*singing*): 'Sniff, Brothers, Sniff. Sniff, Sisters, Sniff, Sniff Brother, Sniff Sister, Sniff, Sniff, Sniff!'

THERESA (*singing*): 'You gotta smell out witches/You gotta sniff and how/You gotta point the finger,/You gotta take the vow/To smell, sniff, point—the time is now! And sniff, sniff, sniff, sniff.'

Lights out to singing and sniffing which quickly mingles with screams as we glimpse through stray gleams of light, the torture instruments being trundled into position.

SCENE XI

Lights up on the Torture Chamber with its door at the top of the stairs Up Stage Centre. PRISONERS *are chained to the wall and there is one unconscious inside the Iron Maiden.*

ANTONIO's *feet are encased in a metal torture instrument called 'the boot'.* DR BRAVO *is on the Wheel and* RAFAEL *is stretched unconscious on the Rack.*

DR BRAVO: Ha' I been dead since Mars and Jupiter crossed? I casn't hear my heart beat pitti-pat-pitti-pat. Only the sound o' air passing through the fluid i' my trachea. Am I dying or is 't my birthday? I want a second opinion!

    He dies as ALCALA *enters from the arch Stage Left, followed by* GOMEZ *gnawing a meat bone.*

ALCALA: Every prison from here t' Seville's full o' suspect witches and more coming daily. We've jus' too much t' do. 'Tis no way t' run a torture chamber. (*He staggers accidentally against the Iron Maiden, the* PRISONER *inside gives a brief pierced cry as the lid slams shut.*) See, that wouldst not've happened if I wasn't so tired.

GOMEZ (*heating a long needle*): We're being paid an extra two ducats a session. Every new suspect means money in our breeches.

ALCALA: But what o' our reputation? T' tickle a true confession from a relapsed sinner takes time and patience, now we've t' gouge 't out, quick and bleeding. Standards're collapsing, Gomez. We're turning this house o' truth into a butcher's shop. I'll go brain-mad wi'out our integrity as craftsmen.

GOMEZ: Ours isn't a craft, but a trade. Our profit lies in bulk. (*He takes red-hot needles from the brazier.*) Who cares about the quality o' the pain, so long as 't *hurts*?

ALCALA: I do! I do!

    Humming to himself, GOMEZ *exits with the hot needles through the archway Stage Left. Furious,* ALCALA *picks up a bucket of water and throws it over* RAFAEL *on the Rack.*

ALCALA: Didst hear him, Master Morra? My son Gomez. He defies mè and all I stand f'. I've raised him since he was a babe. His mother left me twenty years ago. The stigma o' me being Third Assistant Torturer. She said a man o' my age and experience shouldst've been First Assistant at the least. Complained I lacked ambition and left, boot and baggage. Now I'm Chief Torturer and my son's going from me too. Life turns opposite t' what we expect. Oh Gomez, my son, my son!

RAFAEL: Sons ne'er listen t' their fathers and're hung up by the hair and stretched f' 't. He's blind now t' thy virtues, but he'll come back t' you. All know you're a good man, honest, generous, kindly at heart.

ALCALA: What makes you say that?

RAFAEL: Fear.

ALCALA (*laughing*): You'll be the death o' me.

RAFAEL: That's my line, Sir.

ALCALA: Oh, I'll burst me buttons. (*To* ANTONIO.) Didst e'er hear such wit, Monsieur Limpy . . .? (ANTONIO *groans;* ALCALA *turns the screw on his boot;* ANTONIO *cries out.*) Ha' you bewitched His Majesty, Monsieur?! (*He turns the screw again.*) Doest believe in God?!

ANTONIO (*fainting*): Only if he dances.

ALCALA: Tight-arsed sodomite.

   The Inquisitor-General VALLADARES *enters Up Stage Centre.* ALCALA *instantly kneels as* VALLADARES *hobbles down in a fury.*

VALLADARES: Heresy! 'Tis all heresy!

ALCALA: Your Eminence, we're hard pressed, is relief coming?
   FROYLAN *enters through the archway Stage Left, wiping his hands.*

FROYLAN: Ah, Your Eminence. (VALLADARES *just glares at him.*) I've been given special dispensation by the Suprema and the Holy Father t' help the Lord's work here.

VALLADARES: Help?! Ten relapsed Jews were taken this

morning but there was no place f' 'em now i' the witch-filled dungeons o' the Inquisition. They had t' be lodged wi' the *civil* authorities! You're wrecking the Church's whole machinery o' repression wi' your damnable witches!

FROYLAN: They must be o'ercome afore all else.

VALLADARES: That's the colour o' your dream, not mine.

FROYLAN: Doesn't Your Eminence believe in the reality o' witches?

VALLADARES: The Inquisitor Salazar declared there were neither witches nor bewitched until they were talked and written about. 'Tis my duty t' protect reputed witches and warlocks from thy inordinate zeal. I'll not let you turn the Spanish Inquisition into an instrument o' malignant persecution. 'Twas created t' save souls f' Paradise.

FROYLAN: Spain and the King's penis lie crushed.

VALLADARES: Both'll rise again when I've burnt the last heretic from the land.

ALCALA: Holy Fathers, you must gi' me a policy decision! We casn't save the immortal souls o' *both* witches and heretics. We haven't the equipment or men.

VALLADARES (*crossing to* ANTONIO): Didst not St Paul tell the Galatians: 'If anyone preached t' you a Gospel besides that which you've received, let him be an anathema'?

He turns the screw on ANTONIO's *metal boot.*

ANTONIO (*screaming*): Yes.

FROYLAN (*crossing to* RAFAEL): Didst not St Paul also say t' the Galatians: 'Who didst bewitch you?'

He turns the Rack tighter.

RAFAEL (*screaming*): Yes.

VALLADARES: Denyer o' efficacious grace!

FROYLAN: Predeterminist!

VALLADARES: *Heretic-fancier!*

FROYLAN: *Witch-lover!*

ALCALA: Your Majesty.

CARLOS *has entered Up Stage Centre.* ALCALA *kneels, the* OTHERS *bow as* CARLOS *stumbles down the stairs.*

CARLOS: Haaaa found whoooo . . .?

VALLADARES: Ask thy Confessor, Sire, 'tis his murky province.

FROYLAN: We've found hundreds, Sire. 'Tis bigger than that. No one's innocent till proved not guilty. Not my lords Torres, Alba, Oropesa, no not e'en the Queen.

CARLOS: The Queeee . . . ahhh, my bowels 're watery. (*Crosses to* DR BRAVO *on the Wheel.*) Hast a physic f' meeee, doctor . . .? (*No reply.*) Your Sovereign speaks . . . Sulking, sir? I'll haaaa no peevish sulking . . . (ALCALA *whispers to him.*) DEAD . . .? (*He staggers back, putting his fingers in his ears.*) I'll not HEAR 't . . . (*To* RAFAEL.) TTTom, is he ddddd . . .?

RAFAEL (*gasping*): He's dead, Sire. And truth t' tell I too feel like going where the smallest is no smaller than the rest. *Honk* . . .

ALCALA (*laughing*): *Honk.*

No one else laughs and he stops immediately as PONTOCARRERO *enters Up Stage Centre and comes stiffly down the steps.*

CARLOS: YYYour EEE we draw closer t' it, s' jus' ahead. Weee finding more, catching new witches on the wing e'ery second. We squeeze and sweat 'em out.

PONTOCARRERO: Yet no improvements're visible in you or the State, Sire. Spain festers and the world waits f' you t' choose your successor.

CARLOS: 'Tis the wwwitche'ss SPELL. Casn't raise up armies, heirs or penises till broken.

PONTOCARRERO: The French Louis's grown impatient. He expected you t' nominate Philip Bourbon; 'tis why he ga' us a good peace. Now he's forming another alliance wi' the English and low Dutch. This time there'll be no 'scape.

CARLOS: 'Snot my fault. My Confessor knows. I'm bewitched.

PONTOCARRERO: Father Froylan's wrong.

FROYLAN: Wrong? Your Eminence has a different reason f' His Majesty's impotence?

PONTOCARRERO: This's Spain. Nothing's different, only worse.

CARLOS: Wooo? Whaa worse than being bewitched?

PONTOCARRERO: Being *possessed*.

CARLOS: Pooo . . .?

PONTOCARRERO (*producing a book*): The learned Zacharias on possession. (*Reading.*) 'The possessed 've swollen tongues that loll from their mouths, weep wi'out knowing why, talk little sense and oft times fall senseless'.

    CARLOS *snatches the book.*

FROYLAN: I saw to 't no daemon entered His Majesty. The evil's outside, not inside. Take my word, Sire, you're bewitched not possessed.

CARLOS (*reading the book with difficulty*): 'The possessed're afflicted wi' sudden terrors', *ahh, ahh*; 'imitate wild animals', *grrr*; 'speak strange tongues', *vidi, vici, veni* . . .

FROYLAN: Sire, I personally guarded you wi' crucifix and trident from any possible daemonic penetration.

PONTOCARRERO: You forget Satan couldst've penetrated His Majesty when Father Motilla was his Confessor and the succuli's lain dormant in him since.

VALLADARES: 'Tis thy necromantic meddling's stirred the succuli t' life, Father! If 'tis proven I'll ha' you staked and burning afore you canst chant another Pater Noster. Your Eminence's t' be congratulated on exposing a grave error o' a member o' your own Order. The proofs seem pregnant, Your Majesty. If Lucifer attacks a man from wi'out 'tis bewitchment. If he assumes control from wi'in, 'tis deemed possession. You, Sire, casn't control thy limbs or bladder; like that young man Christ found at Mount Tabor, you're possessed o' a foul spirit. Your shield o' faith's cracked and you stand ball-naked 'gainst the dark. You didst not protect the Faith from heretics, faith didst not protect you from the Devil. You showed no zeal f' God, didst not scorch His doubters. 'Twas weakness in you and Satan entered through that same gate. The cause's in you, Sire, though you're not the cause.

FROYLAN: No, 'tis the witches, 'tis outside wi' the witches! You've heard 'em confess to 't, Sire. You're bewitched.

PONTOCARRERO: Read Zacharias, Sire, feel the nail in thy throat, the claw in thy belly. You're possessed.

CARLOS: Casn't seee? I can see by my superior middle-brain . . . I'm not possessed . . . Not bewitched . . . 'Tis worse than worse. (*Trembling, he shuts the book.*) I'm bewitched and possessed *both.*

PONTOCARRERO
VALLADARES
FROYLAN
ALCALA
} (*groaning*): Both?!

CARLOS: Help mmmmm. (*He staggers to the chained* PRISONER.) III'm assailed, OUT beyond and INNER too. (*Clutches his stomach.*) Abounding . . . abounding . . . (*To* ANTONIO.) Monsieur MMM 'tis noon and I've no eyelids! Pray f' me. (*To* RAFAEL.) TTTom TTToom jelly knots inside me! Pray f' me. 'Tis in the King now. Lord, saaa save him from evil, purefy his water and his flesh . . . away . . . aaaawww . . . (*Claws his stomach.*) Whaaa o' me now, whaaa o' Spain? I command thee pray f' us . . . only praaa . . .

He collapses on his knees Down Stage Centre, FROYLAN *and* ALCALA *kneel beside him.* PONTOCARRERO *gestures graciously to* VALLADARES *to lead the prayer. The lights fade slowly.*

VALLADARES: The King's bound t' God's throne wi' a gleaming chain. Pray f' him. Pray f' him. His sins stain the coming years, f' if he sows bad seeds now 'tis future Kings who'll reap bitter harvests. But if he sows no seeds, 'tis worse, f' authority and submission're the twin poles on which Jehovah turns the world and wi'out an heir the King's no longer its standing pillar. 'Tis heresy 'gainst the Church who anointed him, rebellion 'gainst God. Pray f' him. Pray f' him. Satan's in him now; made easy entrance f' he was already touched and weakened, like his subjects, by that foul disease called reason. Oh man needs belief not reason! F' when he discovers the reason f' things he loses the merit o' faith. Gi' us back our faith, Lord; our prejudices! Nothing's more vital than our prejudices, those opinions we accept unexamined. Wi'out prejudices no religion, no morality, no submission. We hunger f' the blessings o' blind ignorance, Lord! We pray. We pray. F' by the sins o' rulers, nations're punished, so we pray f' our salvation, Lord, and the salvation o' our Sovereign lord. Kings stand high, exposed t' blasts that pass o'er the lower valleys. Ha' mercy on our liege, Carlos, who feeds us wi' the sincerity o' his heart and guides us wi' the wisdom o' his head. Now he must be cleansed pure, that we might continue t' love and praise him. F' in loving and praising him, we love and praise thee, Lord, f' he's thy true representative, the very image o' thy monarchy o'er all creation. Et benedíctio Dei Omnipoténtis Patris et Filii . . .

As VALLADARES *kneels with the* OTHERS, *a plain-song chorus is heard singing hoarsely.* 'Praise my soul the King of Heaven./ To his feet thy tribute bring;/Ransomed, healed, restored, forgiven,/Who like we his praise should sing./Alleluja! Alleluja! Praise the everlasting King.'

A chorus of bloodstained COURTIERS *emerge from the archway Stage Left carrying their chains and candles. They are led by* BELEPSCH *with needles sticking out of her arms, a broken* ALBA *and* MONTERREY, *and* TORRES *with his eyes black and bleeding. Whilst* RAFAEL *honks wildly,* ANA *joins them and all kneel and sing:* 'Father-like he tends and spares us/Well our feeble frame he knows,/In his hands he gently bears us,/ Rescues us from all our foes,/Alleluja! Alleluja!/Widely does his mercy flow.'

The candles are snuffed out. There is now only a Spot on CARLOS *praying.* RAFAEL's *ironic honking is heard above the unseen Chorus.* 'Angels help us to adore him,/Ye behold him face to face:/ Sun and moon bow down before him,/dwellers all in time and space./Alleluja! Alleluja! Praise with us the God o' Grace.'

RAFAEL's *honking is finally choked off.*

B—5*

SCENE XII

Lights up on the Throne Room where all are still praying silently.
CARLOS *whispers to* ANA.

CARLOS: I always pray wi' my eyes open so I canst hear whaaa I say.

ANA: It gi's us a chance t' talk, Carlos.

CARLOS: Taaa . . .? Wha taaa . . .?

ANA: Jus' talk, Carlos. Not big talk, jus' a little small talk.

CARLOS (*nods eagerly*): Jus' taaa, jus' jus' . . . Talk. Yes.

> ANA *opens her mouth but finds she has nothing to say.* CARLOS *is about to speak, but frowns dimly instead.* ANA *tries again but thinks better of it.* CARLOS *has a thought but immediately loses it. As they struggle with increasing desperation an* ATTENDANT *enters with a message for* PONTOCARRERO. *He reads it and crosses still on his knees to* CARLOS.

PONTOCARRERO: Sire, the abscess's burst. I ha' t' report a riot,

CARLOS: Wheeee . . .?

PONTOCARRERO: The Plaza Mayor. A woman complained she'd no bread f' her six children. An official told her she shouldst castrate her husband. (ANA *giggles.*) But both he and the joke died the death. He was torn t' pieces. His audience lacked humour as well as bread.

CARLOS: Whaaa . . .?

PONTOCARRERO: Their distress's more than empty bellies Sire . . .

ANA: 'Tis Father Froylan's new-style witch-hunts.

VALLADARES: The people want a return t' traditional *heresy*-hunts.

PONTOCARRERO: They're unsettled by rumours o' your possession, Sire. Show thyself t' their representatives, and let 'em see their King's still in full possession o' his wits.

CARLOS: Satan claws meee . . .

> *The polished Capucin Friar,* MAURO TENDA, *traditionally*

dressed in cowled habit and cord round his waist, enters Stage Right carrying crucifixes and bowing. TWO MONKS *follow behind.*

PONTOCARRERO: Sire, 'tis thy exorcist extraordinary, Friar Mauro Tenda.

CARLOS: Whaaa . . . ?

ANA: My brother John William's certain you and all the Catholic crowned heads o' Europe 've been possessed f' years. 'Tis why he's sent you *the* most fashionable o' all exorcists.

CARLOS: QQQuick the Devil waits.

    CARLOS *rises. So do the* OTHERS.

FROYLAN: Sire, I must humbly protest this foreign friar's presence. 'Tis a slur on me and the whole nation. Spain's ne'er lacked men who canst cast out daemons.

TENDA: But none wi' my occult knowledge o' the Prince o' Evil and his fashionable ways.

FROYLAN: What?! Who discovered and named the four Kings o' Hell; Uriens o' the East, Pymon o' the West, Egyn o' the North and the Southern Amayon?

PONTOCARRERO: Father, there's no time f' a recital o' your academic triumphs. His Majesty wants whatso'er's lurking i' his breast plucked out afore I return wi' some o' his disturbed subjects. Wi' thy permission, Sire.

    CARLOS *nods impatiently and* PONTOCARRERO *exits backwards bowing whilst* TENDA *and* FROYLAN *give their crucifixes to the* TWO MONKS.

FROYLAN: 'Tisn't fair, Sire. Haven't I always gi'en satisfaction?

TENDA: Yet you couldst not determine whether your King was possessed, bewitched or both? A diagnosis any apprentice-exorcist couldst've made. Wi' thy permission, Sire, let me show you the new fashionable method o' determining Satanic presence, by what we call 'controlled experiment'. (*Taking off a silver Cross around his neck he swings it in front of* CARLOS's *eyes.*) F' too long exorcism and daemonology've been bedevilled wi' brute superstition. But this's the Year o' our Lord 1699; watch how we test f' evil. Watch . . . watch . . .

(CARLOS's *gaze is transfixed on the Cross.*) In the name o' Jesus Christ reveal thyself, Satan! Pinch his left hand . . . (CARLOS's *left hand twitches and he yelps.*) Satan, put his left leg out . . . (CARLOS's *leg jerks out.*) Put his right leg out . . . (CARLOS's *other leg goes out.*) Left leg. Right leg. Left—right—left—right . . . (CARLOS *moves stiff-legged around the room.*) Odd. 'Tis an odd business, 'walking'. Why do we all move forward like that 'stead o' a crabby side-shuffle like this . . .? (*He edges sideways.*) Odd. Ma'am, His Majesty's possessed. I shall now exorcise him.

    CARLOS *lurches blindly round amongst the astonished* COURTIERS.

FROYLAN: Sire, they seek t' take you from me. Wi'out thy support I'll be crushed. 'Tis a necromatic conspiracy t' protect the witches.

ANA: There's no conspiracy. I'm certain Friar Tenda'll not stop you trying t' call forth the Devil.

TENDA: 'Twill not disturb me if you wish to dabble, Father. *Satan cease.*

    CARLOS *suddenly stops walking and blinks.*

CARLOS: Oh Jesu, I'm cleansed o' the Devil! My shoulders heave, belly exults, breast cries out wi' joy! I'm exorcised! Exorcised!

TENDA: Sire, we haven't started yet.

CARLOS: Whaaa . . .? 'Tis Monday but it shouldst be Good Friday the way I'm being crucified. CCCCleanse me, cccure my occult impotence! Make me an heir! DO'T DO'T.

    FROYLAN *puts on his dark glasses and* TENDA *a pair of white gloves as he guides* ANA *Stage Left to stand behind the small trunk.*

TENDA: Stay back from Satan's line o' fire, Ma'am, during the spearing o' the demons. We'll raise up a barrier his minions casn't leap. (*He takes out a sachet and sprinkles white powder in front of her.*) Salt. Salt saves dead flesh and live souls from corruption. There's reason e'en in magic. (*He sees* FROYLAN *taking out his trident.*) Great Jerome, a Paracelsus Trident!

Why, I haven't seen one o' those f' twenty years past. Now-adays all reputable exorcists spear incubi and succuli wi' a simple Cross. (*He holds up his Cross; a concealed blade springs out from it.*) And darkened glasses, Father? T' protect you from the invisible aura, eh? (*chuckles*) 'tis quite out o' fashion t' see auras nowadays. But if you see auras, you see auras . . . (*Stops chuckling.*) 'Tis no wonder Your Majesty's both bewitched and possessed. Outdated rituals're no defence 'gainst the e'er changing Powers o' Darkness. (*He lifts up the bottom of his habit and tucks it under his waist-cord, leaving his legs bare.*) Your Majesties, forgive this shameful display o' naked knees. 'Tis essential my lower limbs be free. Father I gi' thee first chance t' exorcise the daemons from thy Sovereign's body—if you can.

FROYLAN: If? I've exorcised more daemons than you've had indulgences!

He takes a holy water stoup from one of the MONKS.

TENDA: Hhhhmmm, holy water. I say nothing 'gainst holy water. 'Tis most effective . . . wi' the commoner sort o' possession. But I've found the Devil lurking in men o' rank and blood hath grown somewhat immune to 't. O' course, 't may be different in Spain.

Suppressing his fury, FROYLAN *begins the exorcism.*

FROYLAN: 'Adjúro te, serpens antiqúe, per júdicem vivórum et mortuórum, per factórem tuum, per factórem (*he throws water into* CARLOS's *impassive face with increasing speed*) qui-habet-potestátem-mitténdi-te-in-gehémnam-ut-ab-hoc-fámulo-Dei. (*He throws the last drop of water into* CARLOS's *face;* CARLOS *blinks.*) I knew 't! Satan's not home! No evil lodges in thy breast, Sire. Thou art merely bewitched, not possessed. 'Tis the witches.

TENDA *takes a small bag from one of the* MONKS.

TENDA: Watch and learn, Father. You use old lustral water, I new kidney beans. (*He takes some from the bag.*) Daemons hate 'em worse than water f' they're charged wi' elemental force.

Their colour 's Christ's blood. Their shape, God's lovin' heart. I pepper you wi' seeds o' life t' drive out your dark daemons, Sire. (*He throws the beans at* CARLOS.) 'Exorcízo te immundíssime spíritus omnis incúrsio adversárii omne phantásma omnis légo in nómine Dómini nostri Jesu Christi effugáre ab hoc phásmate Dei!

He flings the last handful of kidney beans hard into CARLOS's *face.*
CARLOS: *Aeeee. Aieeee. Aieeee.*

CARLOS *goes rigid.* TENDA *signals urgently to* ANA.
TENDA: Keep above the salt, Ma'am, the demons're leaping! The incubi and succuli fly off him. Snot green and pusy-yellow demons. There! There!

The COURTIERS *leap away in terror from the demons. Using his Cross as a weapon* TENDA *launches into the 'spearing of the demons': a series of acrobatic dives and somersaults. In the middle of them he shouts urgently to* FROYLAN *who, carried away with excitement, joins in using his trident as a spear.*

They vault and swoop around the immobile CARLOS *and frightened Court in a fantastic display until during one of* FROYLAN's *Nijinsky-like leaps to skewer a high-flying demon,* ANA *deliberately sticks out her foot. The cleric trips and crashes to the floor with a groan.*

TENDA, *who has seized another small bag from one of the* MONKS, *stops immediately in front of* CARLOS. *There is the faint sound of angry, incoherent chanting off as* TENDA *concentrates all his power.*

TENDA: Satan, recéde ergo in nómine Patris et Filii et Spiritus Sancti! (*He flings red powder into* CARLOS's *face.*) By this dried heifer's blood, symbol o' God's fertility—Satan go forth! (CARLOS *remains rigid.*) Satan . . . in God's name . . . I command thee . . . (*Summoning all his strength, he takes a raw egg from the bag and cracks it on* CARLOS's *forehead.*) GO FORTH.

TENDA *sinks back exhausted. As the egg slides down* CARLOS's *face his lower limbs twitch, the light flickers and the chanting grows louder. We can make out certain repeated words, 'Bread . . .*

Death . . . Bread . . . Death . . .' *The light flickers faster as* CARLOS's *limbs quickly jerk out of control and he falls into an epileptic fit.*

ANA *steps forward to help.* TENDA *shouts a warning for her to keep back but too late.* CARLOS *grabs her hand and her limbs immediately shake violently; the seizure seems contagious.*

As ANA's *and* CARLOS's *legs buckle and they fall shrieking in convulsions, four seven-foot-high effigies of children with swollen stomachs and skull-like faces advance on them out of the dark entrances, Stage Right and Left. They are carried by two surly* PEASANTS *in coarse breeches and doublets and an arsenal of knives and pistols stuffed into their belts.* PONTOCARRERO *pushes past them.*

PONTOCARRERO: Your Majesty, these're representatives o' thy loyal subjects who . . .

He stops and with the OTHERS *stares at* ANA *and* CARLOS *writhing on the floor.*

PONTOCARRERO: Er, we seem t' have caught Their Majesties at their prayers. We shouldst not disturb 'em, they're wrestling wi' God.

But the attack has already passed. The light stops flickering. ANA *and* CARLOS *rise as if nothing had happened;* ANA *resting her hand regally on* CARLOS's *arm. Both are in a state of post-epileptic automation as* CARLOS *stares at the effigies.*

CARLOS: Has Christ died that children might starve?

Why shouldst wealth lie in usurer's pockets?

And whole towns made poor t' raise up the merchants' walls?

(They turn bread t' stones; the Devil'd more charity Turning stone's t' bread; 'tis no wonder men worship him)

Why shouldst some ha' surfeit, others go hungry?

One man two coats, another go naked?

Now I see Authority's a poor provider.

No blessings come from 't

No man born shouldst ha' t', wield 't.
Authority's the Basilisk, the crowned dragon,
Scaly, beaked and loathsome.
Born from a cock's egg, hatched under a toad
Its voice is terror, glance, certain death.
Streams where 't drank once, are poisoned
And the grass around turns black.
'Twill make a desert o' this world
Whilst there's still one man left t' gi' commands
And another who'll obey 'em.
Release all suspects!
I'm not bewitched or possessed,
'Cept t' right the wrongs done my people.
I'll show you the good life, if you'll show me pardon
F' not knowing thy needs and miseries.
I raise my hat t' you three times in courtesy.

*As he mimes raising his hat three times, the effigies deflate and
the* PEASANTS *open their mouths at last.*

PEASANTS (*frightened*): *Baa-baa-baa-baa . . .*

ANA: Cow-elephants kneel, stag-beetles buzz,
  Whales like derelict ships, roll on their sides,
          belly t' belly
  And the glow-worm shines as her winged mate, a
          falling star
  Descends on her t' glow together in the dark, then
          gently fade.
  Oh let's burn bright as exploding Novas in the sky,
  And by the light that makes the red rose, red,
  Cry 'love, love, love' as Jermyn cried 'earth, earth,
          earth'
  Oh men, Oh women, Oh fields, Oh sky, Oh sun,
  Christ comes t' gather up our flowers o' love!
  (*Singing.*) 'Clap-a-yo' hands! Slap-a-yo' thigh!
  Halleluja! Hallelujah!/Everybody come along and
  join the jubilee!'

CARLOS
ANA } (*singing to the* OTHERS *as they rise, bleating*): 'Clap-a-yo' hands! Slap-a-yo' thigh! Don't you lose time, don't you lose time,/Come along it's time t' choose right now f' you and me./ On the sands o' time you are more than a pebble,/Remember trouble must be treated just like a rebel . . .'

OTHERS (*singing*): 'Send him t' the Devil!'

ALL (*singing and dancing*): 'Clap-a-yo' hands! Slap-a-yo' thigh! Hallelujah! Hallelujah! Everybody come along and join the jubilee!

As all dance and sing the panel walls revolve and the dead figures of MARIANA, ALMIRANTE, RAFAEL, DR BRAVO *and* MOTILLA *enter and join in with even more strength and liveliness than the living.*

As they repeat the chorus of the song, individual COURTIERS *step forward for a moment.*

BELEPSCH: God be praised. My life-long friendship wi' the Queen's not broken, though my ten fingers are.

TORRES: I'm blinded by his glory. But I thank His Majesty f' making my world real at the last.

MONTERREY: I thank him too, f' showing me that riches're a wax shield 'gainst the sword o' State. Money must be made the very woof and weave o' society so whoso'er attacks a rich man attacks society.

ALBA: E'en in the House o' Pain my rank and privileges were observed. My body's fire-wracked, my mouth blood-filled, but I cry out, 'God save the King!'.

ALL (*singing and dancing*): 'On the sands o' time we will all need each other,/Remember Judas must be treated just like a brother,/Send us all a lover!/Clap-a-yo' hands! Slap-a-yo' thigh . . .'

CARLOS: Man's a lunatic animal
      Unravelling everything in theory
      Tangling everything in practice.
      But the one creature able t' profit from his errors.

I'll profit from mine, do somersaults,
Drop my sceptre, renounce my crown, vacate my
                                                    throne.
The OTHERS *stop singing and dancing.*
We'll live wi'out orders and obediences,
Wi'out limits t' heart and mind.
Oh won't 't be grand t' live then?!

The OTHERS *let out terrified shrieks and flee leaving only the* DEAD *in a menacing semi-circle round* CARLOS. *The light fades.* CARLOS *stumbles as he returns to normal. His bout of post-epileptic automatism has ended.*

CARLOS: Whaaa . . .? Whaaa . . .? Is the breaking day come? (*The* DEAD *make loud sucking noises.*) Whaaa you taking from me? Whaaa you taking from mmmm . . .? Whaaa you taaa . . . (*He becomes weaker, gasping for breath as the sucking noises continue.*) Whaaa you taa aaa . . .? Whaaa yyy . . .? Whaaa . . .? Aaa-aaa-aa . . .

He collapses. The DEAD *retreat slowly backwards from him into the darkness. A funeral bell tolls once.* CARLOS *is dying.*

SCENE XIII

A chorus chants the prayer for the sick: 'Dómine sancte Pater omnipotentes aetérne Deus . . .' Lights come up on the King's Bedchamber shrouded in dark drapes. The four-poster bed is Stage Left, the low table with the white cloth and holy vessels below it and St Isidore's bones in front of the mirror Stage Right.

PONTOCARRERO, FROYLAN *and* ANA *watch the* TWO ATTEN-DANTS *pick up* CARLOS, *who is barely conscious, and undress him whilst* DR GELEEN *mixes medicines from a small medicine chest and* GONGORA, *up Stage Right, consults his star-charts.*

DR GELEEN: Ma'am, His Majesty's had one hundred and thirty-seven bowel movements in the last four hours. His faeces're steamy black; no muscle in 'em.

ANA: What does that mean?

DR GELEEN: He's dying.

ANA: What of?

DR GELEEN: His birth.

A MESSENGER *enters and hands* PONTOCARRERO *a document from his pouch.* PONTOCARRERO *reads it.*

PONTOCARRERO: The Will must be changed. Louis 's finally convinced his grandson'll ne'er inherit the Spanish throne. He's signed a Third Partition Treaty wi' England and the Dutch t' divide the Empire between 'em. Redraft immediately and make Charles o' Austria heir t' the throne.

FROYLAN: Your Eminence, I'm the King's Confessor!

PONTOCARRERO: No longer. I'm willing t' save a loyal secretary from the Inquisitor-General but not a rebellious Confessor. (*He hands him the pouch.*) Then deal wi' all this.

ALBA *enters Up Stage Centre for the nightly ritual, followed by* MONTERREY *and a stumbling* TORRES. *They all carry their small black cushions.*

With a great effort ALBA *kneels on one knee in front of* CARLOS. *The* ATTENDANTS *place the King's insignia, cloak and doublet on his cushion and the enfeebled* ALBA *nearly topples over with the weight. Rising, he staggers out backwards, whilst* MONTERREY *kneels to receive* CARLOS's *shoes. But he is shaking so much with the palsy, they keep falling off the cushion, as he exits backwards. Finally the blind* TORRES *kneels for* CARLOS's *breeches and withdraws with them straight over a chair Stage Centre.* ANA *watches him crash into every piece of furniture and the doors, before exiting.*

ANA: Your Eminence, Carlos must order the end o' this absurd ceremony.

PONTOCARRERO: He canst order a hundred thousand men go die f' him, and they'll die gladly. But t' order 'em to end

one minor social custom's too much, e'en for the King o'
Spain.

ALBA *staggers back carrying the* KING's *nightshirt on his
cushion.* MONTERREY *follows with the curved, pomaded leather
covers for* CARLOS's *non-existent moustache and* TORRES *with the
Royal chamber-pot.*

As ALBA *kneels and the* ATTENDANTS *put the nightshirt on*
CARLOS, MONTERREY *shakes so violently with the palsy that the
pomaded covers fall off his cushion. Whilst bending down to find
them,* TORRES *careers blindly over him, breaking the chamber-pot
in half.* MONTERREY *is still searching for the covers as* TORRES,
*unable to see, puts the half of the chamber-pot with the handle back
on the cushion, and crosses unsteadily to* CARLOS. *He kneels, but
unfortunately with his back to the* KING. *The* FIRST ATTENDANT
*turns him round the right way and he triumphantly lifts up the
remains of the chamber-pot for* CARLOS. *But the* KING *is unable to
make use of it as he clings weakly to the* SECOND ATTENDANT.

PONTOCARRERO *gestures impatiently. The* FIRST ATTEN-
DANT *touches* TORRES *who gets up and proceeds to exit backwards,
straight into the slow-moving* ALBA *and* MONTERREY *still looking
for the lost pomaded covers. Finally unscrambling themselves, they
exit in a row, with* TORRES *in the middle, squeezing through the
doorway bowing and groaning.*

The ATTENDANTS *start to take* CARLOS *to the bed, but he
struggles feebly and screams in fright.* DR GELEEN *has him placed in
the chair Stage Centre and gives him medicine.*

DR GELEEN: 'Twill harden thy faeces, Sire. Dr Bravo prescribed
pills made o' crab's eyes and oil squeezed from bricks. But all
true remedial medicine must be scientific. I've had the innards
o' a freshly killed calf specially prepared, Sire. (*Low to*
ANA.) I fear his sudden collapse may signal a sudden dying.

ANA: His whole life's been one long dying. I casn't believe he's
dying now.

PONTOCARRERO: I can. Spain's starving, the provinces're in
revolt, our enemies're joined ready t' dismember us and we

still've no heir. His Majesty'll die 'cause 'tis the worst possible time t' die.

GONGORA: I fear the malefic Saturn's retrograde in the 10th House.

FROYLAN: 'Tis the witches' revenge.

PONTOCARRERO: Tend t' your papers, you've forfeited all rights.

FROYLAN: Out o' fear! Mea culpa, mea culpa. Oh how the little green devils laughed. I'm a hen-hearted flunky, a kiss-me-arse coward! *I betrayed what was best in me* . . . The papers're in order, Your Eminence.

    PONTOCARRERO *takes a document from him.*

ANA: Carlos, Carlos. Wouldst like damask prunes in milk? 'Tis your favourite. Nothing's certain, Carlos, 'cept Christ's forgiveness.

PONTOCARRERO: And Death's coming. Sign 't, Your Majesty, and make Archduke Charles o' Austria heir t' the Spanish throne.

    As he places the Will and pen and ink in front of him, CARLOS *lets out a loud cry and slumps down in his chair. All react.*

    DR GELEEN *bends over* CARLOS's *chest.*

DR GELEEN: Permission t' listen t' thy heart, Sire!

PONTOCARRERO: Is he dead, or jus' hovering as usual?!

GONGORA: According t' arithmetical calculation the stars say . . .

ANA: You're dismissed from our sight!

GONGORA: No, Ma'am, they don't say that. (*Consults charts.*) Where do they say . . .?

ANA: GO!

    GONGORA *exits, bowing and muttering over his charts.*

DR GELEEN: His heart's faint. Permission t' thump, Sire. (*He hits* CARLOS's *chest a tremendous blow: then listens again.*) He's lost too much 'natural spirit'—that's the life-gi'ing essence that animates our bodies. Permission t' use thy body-servant, Sire? (*He beckons to the* FIRST ATTENDANT.) Bend down, put your open mouth 'gainst His Majesty's open mouth and breathe.

ANA: The cure's fouler than the sickness.

As the FIRST ATTENDANT *breathes into* CARLOS's *mouth, the* KING *revives. But whilst* CARLOS *grows stronger, the* FIRST ATTENDANT *grows weaker.* CARLOS *clutches him fiercely to suck the 'natural spirit' from him.*

The FIRST ATTENDANT *finally collapses exhausted.* DR GELEEN *gestures to the* SECOND ATTENDANT *who drags his companion out Up Stage Centre.*

DR GELEEN: At least 'twill gi' His Majesty time t' receive Extreme Unction and make his peace wi' God.

PONTOCARRERO: Only after he's signed the Will. Rulers must risk God's grace, souls eternal torment, t' save their Empires... (*Presents* CARLOS *with the Will again.*) Sign, Sire, and then return t' the business o' dying.

ANA: Sign and've done wi' 't at last, Carlos.

CARLOS: Whaaa...?

PONTOCARRERO (*quickly reading the Will*): 'In accordance wi' the laws o' these kingdoms, I declare my successor t' be— shouldst God take me wi'out bearing heirs—Archduke Charles o' Austria, who shall not allow the least dismemberment o' these said kingdoms.'

CARLOS *takes the document and* PONTOCARRERO *offers him a pen and ink.* CARLOS *pushes it aside.*

CARLOS: No, I command you, delete the Archduke Charles o' Austria's name. Substitute Philip Bourbon o' France!

ALL: WHAAA...?!

PONTOCARRERO: You're sick, Sire!

CARLOS: No, dying. (*He stands up.*) My mind's a sudden burning glass now life creeps out wi' every breath I take. I feel 't going. *Quick, quick,* I've some six minutes left t' eternity, *quick, quick.*

Taking quick gasping breaths he paces intently whilst the lights grow brighter and brighter.

PONTOCARRERO: Sire, we casn't gi' the throne t' the Frenchman, 'tis against all our traditions, prejudices...

ANA: Austria's our ally.

CARLOS: Only France's strong enough t' hold our Empire together.

PONTOCARRERO: But Louis 's just signed a Treaty o' Partition wi' England and the Dutch t' divide our dominions 'tween 'em.

CARLOS: He'll turn Judas t' get all, rather than a part.

PONTOCARRERO: The rest o' Europe'll ne'er allow France t' inherit the whole Spanish Empire. They'll fight . . .

CARLOS: . . . the War o' the Spanish Succession, 1701–1713. Oudenade, Ramillies, Malplaquet, Blenheim. One million dead. Two million wounded. Western Europe in ruins. But Spain and her Holy Empire'll remain intact, *quick, quick.* Delete and substitute!

PONTOCARRERO: Sire, Sire, I see the logic o' 't, but the logic o' 't makes all that's gone afore meaningless. F' thirty years we've striven t' produce an heir. Austrian, Bavarian, Spanish, only so 'twasn't French. 'Twas the reason f' our sins; the horrors and the pain. Wi' this one blind stroke you make 't all pointless. What o' my broken arm, leg, cries, thuds, 'Oh live and let live'? Is that f' nothing?

ANA: And the deaths o' Father Motilla and my lord Almirante, nothing? Belepsch's white hairs, nothing? My hatred o' the Queen Mother, nothing? NOTHING? All swallowed into nothing!

FROYLAN: Sire, Sire, I fought Satan so's you could procreate, tore him out from senseless flesh—rack, screws, branding irons! If you take the French squab, 'tis all wi'out purpose. The Devil's won and we're lost!

CARLOS: He has, we are. The Lord o' Unreason rules and we stand alone at the mercy o' Chance. The empty Universe's deaf t' our voice, indifferent t' our hopes, crimes and sufferings. It contains no reasons, patterns, explanations. They're words t' soothe soul's terror o' our impotence. My reign's a glorious monument t' futility. Father prepare oil and bread! Physician, mix potions! Your Eminence, DELETE AND SUBSTITUTE!

PONTOCARRERO *takes the Will to alter it*, DR GELEEN
returns to his medicines and FROYLAN *crosses to the table to prepare
Extreme Unction.*

ANA: What o' me?! No more gold crucifixes, fluted silver
diamonds and opals. The Frenchman'll not be beholden t' me
f' his throne. I'll be EX'D. Carlos, Carlos, there's another
way, in this room, that bed, your father Philip at his dying,
danced a goat's gig on your mother and procreated. Carlos,
all nature advises, buzz, buzz. The solitary bees, scolia, masons
and bembex, mount and couple jus' afore they fall dead.
Oh buzz, buzz, Carlos. (*She hysterically starts taking off her
farthingale.*) I'll be thy soft warming pan, Carlos! Buzz. It
takes but a second t' take life and make life, be my loving
chopping boy, Carlos! *Buzz. Buzz.*

As she frantically pulls off her dress, CARLOS *continues pacing,*
PONTOCARRERO *changing the Will,* DR GELEEN *mixing
medicines and* FROYLAN *preparing the oil and bread. Their actions
grow jerkier and faster like a speeded up film under remorselessly
fierce lights.*

CARLOS: *Quick, quick,* afore the light holes my brain . . . (*A light
bulb shatters and* CARLOS *jerks round.*) IIII'm here t' die, 'tis the
ooonly certainty . . . (*Another bulb shatters, then another;*
CARLOS *jerks round and round as the light diminishes.*) IIII'm
pouring AWAY fff . . . (*More bulbs blow: it grows darker;*
CARLOS's *jaw slackens.*) SSSS Isidore's bones ddaaa . . . aaah . . .
arrggh . . . *MammaaAAAA.*

As more lights shatter, he cries out and collapses into the chair.
DR GELEEN *stops mixing his medicine,* FROYLAN *pouring out the
'oil of the sick' and* ANA *ripping off her endless petticoats and all
rush over to him. But* PONTOCARRERO *is there first and thrusts
the Will into* CARLOS's *lap.*

CARLOS: Whaaa . . .?

PONTOCARRERO: It makes Philip Bourbon the next Catholic
King o' Spain. (*He puts the pen into* CARLOS's *enfeebled hand.*)
I was too rigid t' bend t' the obvious, too blinkered t' e'en see

't. Blind! Now I'm left t' convince the new Philip I've always supported him . . . (*Guiding* CARLOS's *hand.*) Sign there, Sire . . .

ANA: No, Carlos! Buzz, Carlos!

But he signs, and as he falls back exhausted, the funeral bell tolls, the doors Up Stage Centre are flung open and a HOODED MONK *carrying a gold Cross aloft enters followed by other* MONKS *with lighted black candles and chanting the 'Miserere'.*

They proceed to remove the furniture, drapes and then the walls themselves, completely dismantling the Bedroom Set. Whilst DR GELEEN *tries to make* CARLOS *drink his medicine,* ANA *tears hysterically at her seemingly endless series of petticoats and* FROYLAN *and* PONTOCARRERO *hurriedly prepare to administer Extreme Unction.*

The gold Cross is lowered for CARLOS *to kiss.* FROYLAN *holds out the bowl of oil.* PONTOCARRERO *dips his thumb into it and makes the sign of the Cross on* CARLOS's *forehead whilst muttering the ritual prayer:* 'Per istam sanctam Unctionem . . .' *Wiping away the oil on* CARLOS *with a small piece of wool, he dries his thumb on the bread.*

TWO MONKS *gently lift* CARLOS, *strip off his clothes and leave him naked except for a dirty loin-cloth.*

The bell tolls and DR GELEEN, FROYLAN *and the* MONKS *exit chanting Up Stage.* ANA *is escorted out by* TWO MONKS, *still tearing in frustration at her petticoats and sobbing.*

ANA: Buzz, Carlos! Buzz, buzz!

PONTOCARRERO *and* CARLOS *are left alone in a Spot, Stage Centre.*

PONTOCARRERO: Sire, you were wrong t' say there's only one certainty that you're here t' die. There's one other—you're here t' die *alone*.

CARLOS *tries to clutch at him, but bowing* PONTOCARRERO *exits backwards into the darkness.*

CARLOS: I command . . . order . . . JJJesu . . . I flow out and into my death . . . dddown the drain o' history . . . howling like a dog i' a dream . . . *aaaaaavvvvaa* . . . there . . . *SEE*.

He gives a final convulsive jerk. Two rolls of narrow, white cloth concealed in his hands snake out across the floor as he falls back dead.

TWO HOODED MONKS *enter out of the darkness Stage Left, tie the ends of the bands of cloth round the dead man's ankles and drag him off as the funeral bell tolls and the Spot fades.*

EPILOGUE

PONTOCARRERO'S VOICE: But our ending's not despair but hope. Not death but life. F' Kings die t' rise again, like our Saviour, t' steal us t' glory, t' lead us out o' darkness into the Caanite light o' a new age: the Age o' Reason. (*Lights slowly up.*) Oh blessed beams. T' see! T' understand! T' delight! The last Spanish Hapsburg's dead, the first Spanish Bourbon's born. No longer Louis XIV's grandson, Duke o' Anjou, Philip o' France, but new crowned—Philip V o' Spain!

Lights up on the Throne Room. The whole Court is assembled. As bells peal a great choir sings an exultant 'Te Deum' and the floor Down Stage Centre splits. PHILIP V *emerges wrapped in a gold cloak and carrying a sceptre. Whilst a mighty anthem plays he makes his way up the rostrum and turns.*

PHILIP V *is another freak, with massive legs and arms, bloated stomach and a small elephant's trunk hanging down over his chest in place of a nose.*

As he lowers himself onto the throne all cry: 'God save the King.' 'The King shall live forever.' PHILIP V *trumpets back loudly in reply and a huge, grinning imbecile's face is projected over the King and the throne.*

The lights fade down to a night sky with stars; the music and sounds dissolve into a cold night wind. Then one by one the stars go out. The wind too finally dies.

Silence. Darkness. Curtain.

THE END